Everyone's Invited

Everyone's Invited

Geoffrey Thomas

Reformation Heritage Books
Grand Rapids, Michigan

Reformation Heritage Books
3070 29th St. SE
Grand Rapids, MI 49512
616-977-0889
orders@heritagebooks.org
www.heritagebooks.org

Printed in the United States of America
22 23 24 25 26 27/10 9 8 7 6 5 4 3 2 1

Library of Congress Cataloging-in-Publication Data

Names: Thomas, Geoff, 1938- author.
Title: Everyone's invited / Geoffrey Thomas.
Description: Grand Rapids, Michigan : Reformation Heritage Books,
    [2022]
Identifiers: LCCN 2021050088 (print) | LCCN 2021050089 (ebook) |
    ISBN 9781601789204 (paperback) | ISBN 9781601789211 (epub)
Subjects: LCSH: Salvation—Biblical teaching. | BISAC: RELIGION /
    Christian Ministry / Evangelism
Classification: LCC BS2545.S25 T46 2022 (print) | LCC BS2545.S25
    (ebook) | DDC 234—dc23/eng/20211117
LC record available at https://lccn.loc.gov/2021050088
LC ebook record available at https://lccn.loc.gov/2021050089

*For additional Reformed literature, request a free book list from
Reformation Heritage Books at the above regular or email address.*

To Dr. Albert N. Martin

Contents

Preface

Dr. Al Martin spoke on the true nature of coming to Christ almost fifty years ago. I have used the structure of his approach, which I still find to be enormously helpful, explaining a lot of the phenomena one sees in the professing church today. Certain sections of this book are his, as they are vital and as relevant as when he first preached them half a century ago. I have added much and changed the focus of this book to address the sympathetic inquirer who desires to know what it means to come to Jesus Christ, the Son of God. I have written it to encourage people on this happy journey to be one with Him. I have dedicated the book to Al Martin, whose trilogy of books on preaching titled *The Man of God* will surely be of lasting value until the end. Without his planting these seeds in my understanding all those years ago, I would not have ventured to share them with the world today.

Won't You Come Now?

My wife and I were walking the grounds of Chiswick House, looking at the lake, the waterfall, a heron, early crocuses, children, and the ubiquitous dogs. A young woman ahead of us let her dog off its lead, and off he ran, exploring the park with all the delight of his newly given liberty. He came to a fork in the road and chose the upper path, while his owner had taken the lower one. As we strolled along after her, we noticed she could see him running here and there, stopping, sniffing, looking around, and she called him from the southern path, "Alfie!" He paid no attention at all and ran on. She called again, "Alfie!" He was far too interested in other things to consider the location of the familiar voice calling his name. She called again, this time louder and more stridently: "Alfie! Come! Come here!" Still no response. The two paths were now going farther apart, and undergrowth and bushes were between her and the dog. Often we lost sight of him. Now she was getting serious about his return to her. She stopped walking and stood, crying loudly with notes of angry concern—"Alfie! Alfie! Come here! Alfie! Come!" He must come. He *had* to come.

The delay presented her with an easy decision. Would she stop her cries and shrug in indifference? Would she think, "Well, if that's his choice, he can please himself. I can do nothing more"? Would she look at my wife and me as we were walking behind her, shake her head, half smile and sigh, saying to us, "You do so much, then they run off. That will be the third dog I've had to give up on"? Would she think, "He has made his mind up. He has chosen to deafen his ears against my commands. He has decided to reject my invitation. What more can I do? He may find his way back to the car or to home, or then he may not. Someone else will find him. Someone may take him in and be a better owner than me. He may end up in a dog shelter and they will offer him to someone else, or else they will have him put down painlessly"? Or would she go after him and search until she had found him?

That issue was a no-brainer for her. Not for a moment did such thoughts rise in her mind. She was not a callous, indifferent dog owner. She could not desert him. She loved her dog, and the thought of losing him was unthinkable. She would go after him. So we saw her pushing through the briars and under-growth to the other path, seeking him, calling all the time, "Alfie! Come here, Alfie!" We lost sight of her but kept hearing her increasingly distant voice calling out, "Alfie! Alfie! Come here, Alfie," until, we presume, she finally found him and rubbed his head reprovingly but lovingly, "You come to me when I call you, you rascal." And as always, by her persistent and determined graciousness, at the end of their stroll, he accompanied her again to the home they shared.

How important it is to come when someone calls us, especially a person with authority, such as a teacher, our commanding officer, our parent, our boss, or a policeman. It is very serious to ignore their words and look away, but it becomes particularly poignant when the person who is calling also loves us dearly—when he or she is the one who intends to do us much good, who will meet our needs and warmly welcome us. As they are saying, "Come to me," they are smiling so cheerfully at us, and all their intentions are honorable, healing, strengthening, and joyful. Will we come, or do we think we know better, turning away?

I believe, along with every other Christian, that the Lord Jesus Christ is the loving Son of God. He is the Word of God incarnate—that is, "made flesh." He is that very God and Lord who for centuries was speaking to men and women by His servants the prophets. Through them all He'd been saying, "Return to God!" But when the Lord Christ came (He who was and remains as much a man as any of those prophets were), He stood among men as one who was full of grace and truth—bone of our bone, flesh of our flesh, found in fashion as a man. He showed to everyone who observed Him the character of God, teaching us about Himself while continuing to be the archetypal man. All we need to know about Him is recorded in the Gospels of Matthew, Mark, Luke, and John.

While our Lord spoke to men and women, He often employed one very simple word: "Come!" In other words, He is saying to us, "You're not anywhere near Me or following Me. In fact, you're moving farther away from Me. I want you to come to Me. Before you do anything else—before making any resolutions, before discovering totally satisfying answers to every one of your questions, before studying all other religions and weighing up all their claims—there is one thing you must do. Give absolute priority to this: come, just as you are, to Me, finding out more about Me, learning who I am and what I do for people who come, and what it will mean to go through life day by day with Me, facing the challenges and the privileges of the future with My loving counsel and help. Don't go it alone. Why should you? You must come to Me, and don't delay."

ONE

To Whom Is Christ Saying "Come"?

Some of the most familiar words ever spoken by the Lord Jesus Christ are these: "Come to Me, all you who labor and are heavy laden, and I will give you rest. Take My yoke upon you and learn from Me, for I am gentle and lowly in heart, and you will find rest for your souls. For My yoke is easy and My burden is light" (Matthew 11:28–30).

The words are not some sweet platitude suitable for embroidering on a bookstore throw pillow. The Lord Christ at this time was confronting cities where He had raised the dead, healed every sick person, and taught His most unforgettable sermons, but many in these places considered Him a seven-day wonder and went on in their lusts and anger. This was just an inconvenient time for them to think about religion and consider coming to Him. Coming is never convenient.

So these familiar words were spoken in this context of cities, nations, and people who were weary of themselves, experiencing an unrest of their own making. But the

Son of God was at peace. He knew that men were not in control of the future; God was in charge. He was no spectator, wringing His hands helplessly as He saw all that was going on. He was hiding truth from the sophisticates of this world while revealing true wisdom to people who seemed mere babes. This is the context into which the Lord Jesus Christ spoke these great words. What He said to all was this: "Come! You must come to Me and find real rest."

Jesus's warnings, commands, and invitations are totally sincere to all who hear them. He is not tantalizing. He does not flirt with men, waiting for the first show of interest and then giggling, moving on!

Who may respond to this invitation? We can answer it in a few ways.

Jesus Sincerely Beckons the Worst of the Human Race to Come

Jesus asks the chief criminals and the most guilty sophisticates—in short, the very last men and women you'd expect—to come to Him. You might have expected that Christ would desire good people to come and follow Him, not rotten stinkers! But consider with me for a moment the parable of the great supper, recorded in Luke 14. It tells us that a certain man laid out a huge banquet. He sent his servants out to invite all his friends to come to it, but many of them, hearing the invitation, made excuses and refused to come. When the man heard of their response, he was angry and sent his servants out again and told them to immediately hurry into the

streets and "bring in here the poor and the maimed and
the lame and the blind…. Go out into the highways and
hedges, and compel them to come in" (Luke 14:21, 23).
Who is to come to this banquet? How does the master
describe the people they must invite?

The Poor

You may be poor in circumstances, but that is no bar-
rier to prevent your coming. You shiver in rags and
are destitute of bread to eat, but today and now "the
poor have the gospel preached to them" (Matthew 11:5).
You are poor spiritually, lacking in faith, in virtue, in
good works. You have no grace and, what is worse, no
hope. I want to tell you that my Master is sending you
a gracious invitation today to come. Though you may
have nothing but threadbare clothes on your back, and
though your own righteousness is as filthy rags, it's you
whom I invite first of all to come to Christ.

The Maimed

You may feel you are deformed and ugly, unlovable,
an outsider, unable to work, ashamed to meet people, a
worthless loner, an object of pity. You may have thought
to yourself, "Who would want someone like me?" And
so you think that if you went to church and turned to
religion it would be a further sign of weakness—but
you want to show you are tough! Worse, when you've
tried to do good, evil is active in you and round about
you, turning you away from it. You are "maimed" and
have given up on anything that could bring you near

to God. You feel you simply could not walk along the narrow path to life alongside all those good and holy people because you are deformed. But more than that, you find it quite impossible to obey when Christ says, "Come to Me." You feel your utter inability to turn to Him. And as for pleasing almighty God? That is simply not the way you think. But if you will hear me, then it is to you I am sent to assure that however maimed, impotent, helpless, ugly, or worthless you might feel, if you do this one thing—calling on the name of the Lord and coming to Him, saying, "Lord, here I am. Help me!"—then even your maimed life will be transformed.

The Lame

You limp along in life, sometimes feeling a bit religious but at other times utterly rejecting religion as irrelevant and simply boring, with nothing to offer you. The progress you feel you've made in the Christian religion might seem to have been one or two little limping steps forward—and then three back. You have made an embarrassingly tiny advance, with scarcely any strength in it. You might occasionally feel a little religion but then are bought by the smiles of irreligious men and frightened by their frowns. So your life is one lame limp. Yet God might see it differently—that He has brought people to help you, to encourage you to think of coming to Jesus Christ. Maybe one of them gave you this book.

Consider your ways. Each day brings you nearer to your death. Every person is urged to prepare to meet God! And how best to meet Him? The only way, and certainly the first step, is to come to Christ. That is your priority now; bow before His Son. End this lame walk through life, this movement without style and vigor, this sad kind of shuffle. You are neither setting God always before you and serving Him nor setting the world before you and doing and believing the same as everyone in your sphere of influence. You are thinking there has to be more to life than the crowd. You are unhappy with the worldling but also unhappy with the Christian, like the big ball bearing in a pinball machine shooting off everything, not knowing what and where you will be going next. That is not life! Limping man, take a stand and choose this day whom you will serve! Make it this mighty, loving Savior. Come to Jesus and be welcomed with open arms!

The Blind

Perhaps you are someone who does not see God's glory in the harvest moon, the sunset, the dawn as the sun rises over the sea, the majestic mountain, the star-filled night, the rainbow, and God's beautiful creatures. There before your eyes in the world above and around you are being displayed some of the magnificent attributes of God, such as His power, but you cannot see them. You are blind. The life of Jesus Christ is recorded in the Gospels, but you are blind to His deity. You cannot see the corruption of your own heart and conscience and imagination, but, alas, you cannot face the state of your heart either. You refuse to be persuaded of this reality: that God so loved the world He gave His only begotten

Son, that whoever puts his trust in the Lord Jesus will not perish but have eternal life. You keep saying, "I can't see it." You are blind to the loveliness of God and so have no desire for Him, but He has sent me to assure you that He is inviting you personally, this moment, to come to Him for sight and reality and the life of heaven in your life on earth. Can't you say simply to God, "Open my eyes"?

Come! If I could, I would compel you to come. I am using whatever eloquence and powers of description and earnestness that I possess to constrain you to come to God the Son without any more delay, just as you are now, and begin to live. It is urgent that you come now to Jesus Christ! He is saying to you, "Come!"

Every Ordinary Person without Exception Is Urged to Come

The Lord Almighty really does want all who hear Him—all men and women, young and old, all the world over—to come to Him. He would have every person turn from their idols and decide that from now on they were going to come and continue following Him. He is able to give every one of them rest. Whoever we meet in life, whoever we come across in the providence of God, we should not think for a fleeting moment that we possess no good news for that particular person. What they have been and done does not prohibit them from receiving the benefits of coming to Jesus Christ, who nods and says, "Yes, you too, will you please come to Me?" We have a welcoming Savior to reveal to people. We have a gospel message—that is, good news to share with all whom we meet—and we can't keep silent. Whoever you are and whatever you have been and done, God does not want you to perish. Rather, He wants you to come to His Son Jesus Christ for redemption.

God commands all men everywhere to repent. Every Christian believes those words because they are in the Bible, spoken by an apostle of Jesus Christ. What is the character of this universal command? Can I compare it to the orders a sergeant-major gives on the parade ground to two hundred soldiers? "Right, left, right, left! Right turn! Stop! Attention! Stand at ease!" Is this how the Lord commands men to turn? As an adversary? Clinically? Loudly monotone? Inviting no questions or protests? "Attention! Repent and come to Me!" It is certainly not.

We have a patient, beseeching Savior. There is a note of pleading. He is highly concerned with the response He can see. "Turn! Turn! Why will you perish? I take no pleasure in the death of the wicked." God does not rub His hands with delight as many refuse His mercy. No! Until their last breath Jesus's desire is that they should come to Him. Even in his final hour of life, dying nailed to a cross, a criminal worthy of crucifixion for the heinous acts he had inflicted on men and women was enabled to come to Christ, saying to Him, "Please never forget me! Have me in Your thoughts and consider me with mercy!" Our Lord said, "Today you will be with Me—in paradise!" The Lord hesitates from treating all men and women as they deserve. He waits! He is patient and persistent, even till the last hour. He shrinks from executing a swift judgment. He earnestly desires for each person to end his or her hostility of unbelief toward God. His pleasure comes from seeing them pause and think. He sees them asking themselves whether this life of stubborn resistance to Jesus Christ is helping them and preparing them for death. His joy is in seeing them beginning to speak hesitatingly and almost embarrassed to this One whom they barely know, asking Him if He will possibly help them, confiding that they feel they need Him, but all this "religion" is uncharted territory. "Mercy!" Whenever He hears such a cry, He leaps for joy, and all heaven celebrates with Him. No angel can give Him the delight that a very evil man can give when he begins to turn and come to Christ. Jesus is not like us, saying, "Well, I warned you, didn't I? You had it coming to you!" No, He is patient, waiting, forgiving with joy and enthusiasm, condemning with reluctance. Here is love as vast as the ocean.

That is the basis of His delight—His love for the human race. It is the love of its Creator who first made mankind in His own image. How can He ever stop loving us? He cares for the human race; He is full of benevolence even toward individuals, families, and societies whose mode of operation grievously is one of disdain for Him. So, the most godlike thing we can do is to show our enemies love by telling them of a Savior who has been the author of every lovely thing they have ever experienced. This God sent His Son to make an atonement sufficient not only for the Jews but for the entire world. He commands softly, tenderly, irresistibly to all kinds and states of men and women to be reconciled to Himself. He will welcome every prodigal son with open arms, whispering in his ear that He'll never let him go again. He will grant him all the privileges of being a child of God, making him His heir. He will tell the angels, "Don't you know that this was My lost son and now he's found? He was dead, but he is alive again," and heaven will be thrilled and full of joy at the news.

That is why He is so patient with the world. He does not want it to be destroyed but rather desires that people should turn and come to His Son. He wants all men to be saved and come to a knowledge of the truth. When Paul tells the young minister, Timothy, those very words, he is inferring that all people—those in authority, chief executioners, the governor of a prison, adulterers, traitorous tax collectors working for the occupying power, army officers and tyrants—are embraced by God's loving, sincere desire for their salvation (1 Tim. 2:1–4). That is the reason He sends His servants to bring the message of the gospel. He also commands us to pray for our unbelieving family, our community, our nation, and our world because our praying for their redemption is pleasing to God, and we are to assure them that if any of them believe on His Son, they will be saved.

Their present rejection grieves the Savior, as He once displayed when preaching to Jerusalem. He said to its citizens, "How often would I have protected you from the forces that would destroy you? I would have been like the mother hen sending out a warning noise to her chicks to run quickly under the shelter of her wings because of the hawk circling about them in the sky, ready to swoop and kill. Come to Me for safety! All of you come now!" The psalmist also speaks of this divine love: "He shall cover you with His feathers, and under His wings you shall take refuge" (Psalm 91:4). But when the Lord Jesus was confronted with the desolate indifference of that city, He groaned, "O Jerusalem! Jerusalem!" He displayed His love for rebel sinners by laying down His life for them on the cross.

Yes, but before that He had shown His affection by living for them, and in their midst, walking the land from end to end, not having a place to call His own where He could rest His head. He preached, healed, prayed, sighed, counseled, answered questions, debated, and pointed out the two ways before them all: one narrow that led to life and one broad that led to destruction. He set before them Himself—the way, the truth, and the life, the only way of coming to the Father. He said to them all, "Come to Me!"

Someone has pointed out that God had sent Moses to instruct His people, Isaiah to proclaim good news, Jeremiah to weep, but then at the right time He came Himself—in person, in the flesh, visible, audible, wooing, warning, pleading, offering rest to all the world's weary. He was willing for them all to come to Him, but they were unwilling. He pleaded with them to come, but they refused. They will bear the whole responsibility for their decisions and actions. They will get no injustice in the destruction that is the destination of the broad road. They will get exactly what they have chosen: endless life without God. He sincerely wants all people to come to His Son as the Lamb of God who will remove the guilt of their sin and be their sovereign protector. Come, come, come!

Every Religious Person Is Being
Reminded of What It Is to Come to Christ
Some Have a Counterfeit Understanding
of What Coming to Christ Means

People must know what coming to Christ means. We live in an age in which religious decisions, rituals, ideas, and feelings are commonplace. There are ceremonies, courses, classes, speeches, phrases, and much else. Assurance is then given to those who are taking part, inferring that henceforth in life and death all will be well between them and God. But wait a moment! What if they have actually been deceived in a decision as crucial as this? Maybe you have not. Maybe all is well with your soul and God. I hope that this is so, but didn't Jesus warn us of the activities of false prophets? Could you have been influenced by a "wolf dressed in sheep's clothing"? Could you have been sold the counterfeit by a shining face, twinkling eyes, and a sincere voice? Then will it not be a mercy for this book to have been brought to you so that you might discover the difference between the counterfeit and the genuine? If you had once been sold a costly painting but then discovered what was hanging on your wall was a worthless forgery, wouldn't you be angry that men had deceived you? Don't we know that there are religious charlatans in our groaning world and that many have been led astray by them? That is surely undeniable, and if in fact you've been deceived, then won't you increasingly bless God that you discovered it before it was too late?

What an extraordinary church the congregation in Corinth was! What gifts and leaders and growth! Yet their founder and pastor wrote to them, saying, "Examine yourselves as to whether you are in the faith. Test yourselves. Do you not know yourselves, that Jesus Christ is in you?" (2 Corinthians 13:5). My concern in this little book is to show you what it really is to come to Christ in the way that the Bible describes as a genuine and valid spiritual experience, one that will stand a divine evaluation. I am hoping that if the foundation of your faith is weak and insufficient that God will show you through His Word and that He will then show you the good and blessed way.

You ask, "Isn't that a cruel thing, to challenge and shake a religious life?" No, it is not cruel, any more than it was cruel for the meek and gentle Lord Jesus to warn the Pharisees that they were mistaken in building their lives on a foundation of rituals, of getting the best places at feasts, of self-exaltation, of establishing a regime of fastings, of scrupulously tithing everything, of the pretense of making long prayers. What a heavy burden was such a religion of restriction! They sincerely believed such a foundation displayed to everyone that they had truly turned to God and were safe. But in reality they were laying no foundations for any religious security at all. They were erecting a monstrous edifice in which men lived who devoured widows' houses and who itched to hear praises and greetings from ignorant people as they walked through the marketplace. That is no foundation on which to build a future and an eternity, and so the Lord Christ kindly and bravely warned them, yet they continued to be sincere and zealous evangelists for their beliefs, knocking on doors and seeking to gain converts. They were blind guides to others walking in darkness. The sweetest thing that can happen to anyone who has been deceived by false religion is to discover that they have been led astray. Then they can act, read, think, pray, and lay a new foundation on the work and words of the Lord Jesus Christ. What a blessing I might be to you if I destroyed unbiblical convictions you may have about what it means to come to Christ.

Have you heard Christ's words, that the one who comes to Him will in no way be cast out? Have you been persuaded that you have come to Him? That is great, but have you ever taken the time to ask what the Bible means by coming to Christ? Or have you imposed your own meaning on the words of the Lord Jesus? "I have come to Him," you claim, "and so He won't cast me away." I hope you have already come in deed and in truth, but what if you have never come to Him in the way the Lord Himself has set out as a real coming? Don't be afraid of examining yourself. One thing we know about the Lord Jesus is that He loves His own people with an everlasting love, and His intention is that we enjoy His love. He is not in the business of creating floundering doubters. He wants you to know that you are precious to Him, that you are His and He is yours, and that you have really come to Him. No one has been damned for self-examination, but millions have been damned for presumption.

Every New Convert Must Understand
Clearly What It Is to Come to Jesus
Perhaps you spent years of your life in vanity and pride, indifferent to the Christian religion, self-centered, plea-sure loving, just a sleeping sinner! If you are no longer like that, I rejoice. It means you are no longer uncon-cerned about God and untroubled at the state of your never-dying soul, indifferent about heaven and hell, death and judgment. A friend has talked to you, you heard a preacher, you read a tract, or somehow in a mys-terious way your conscience was stirred and a desire for God grew in your inner life. You began to catch glimpses of the beauties of Jesus Christ. There grew a longing to know Him, to have the Lord for yourself and obtain peace with God—these things have become of vital importance to you. You have been awakened by the Spirit of God to the reality and importance of spiri-tual issues. More than that, you were not at peace until you found a congregation where the climactic aspect of worship was explaining the Bible and applying its

truth to your life, challenging and encouraging you and showing you more clearly the Lord Jesus Christ.

These early years are a crucial period in your life. It is quite possible you can't pinpoint that exact day when you had assurance that Jesus Christ was your Savior. That is quite common. You gained a gradual assurance over a period of time in which you began to realize increasingly that you had become a true Christian and had really come to Christ. You now find yourself concerned with having a growing relationship with God. You are attending religious meetings, reading the Bible, and talking to your family and friends about your new interest in religion. This is a crucially important time of self-understanding. The world will at first show you good-natured tolerance. You are not the first person to get interested in religion, and your family and friends will look at you and think kindly, "Well, the jury is still out about this religion business." You are sure to become a target for the fiery darts of the Evil One. He will want to confuse you about what is happening. He will seek to drive you in the wrong direction. There can be no greater help to you during this time than understanding something as basic as what it means to come to the Lord Jesus Christ.

All Who Have Truly Come to Christ
Will Never Tire of His Invitation
Those who have been called by Christ will never grow tired of singing such hymns as this one by Horatius Bonar:

> I heard the voice of Jesus say,
> "Come unto me and rest,
> Lay down, thou weary one, lay down
> Thy head upon My breast"
>
> I came to Jesus as I was,
> Weary, and worn, and sad.
> I found in Him a resting place
> And He has made me glad

God began a good work in your life when He first
stirred within you concern about your condition and
caused you to realize that the Lord Jesus was in fact
the Son of God, full of grace and truth. You may have
known Him as long as I have, and that first assurance
was given to me way back in 1954. Do you and I still
need to grasp what coming to Christ means? "Yes, of
course!" you will say. "I love to hear the story of what
the Son of God did and how people can come to Him
and find Him as their teacher and their Lord." There is
a hymn which says that those who best know this truth
"are hungering and thirsting to hear it like the rest." The
fruit of understanding what it is to come to Christ more
clearly will be renewed gratitude for the marvelous
work God wrought in your life when He drew you to
His Son. I hope that before you finish this little book
you will be pressed down on your face expressing gratitude to your loving heavenly Father. May you be lost in
wonder, love, and praise for all that He did in choosing
you in eternity, giving you to His Son, sending Him to
live and die for you, commissioning the Holy Spirit to

draw you to the Lamb of God in the way of a saving trust, and keeping you up to this moment.

I long for the Lord to make you glad as you read these words. I truly hope this little book will be not only a message of instruction to produce new gratitude to God but also a word of clarity for you to help others who are floundering in their religion and have never been instructed in the true meaning of coming to the Lord Jesus Christ. So let me conclude this chapter by reemphasizing these truths: that the worst of people need to know they are invited to come to Christ, that the most fiendish past behavior does not prevent them from coming, that all religious people need to know and understand this truth, and that new believers especially will find it most helpful. Finally, those who have walked with God for decades and are full of the hope of heaven can still find these words of Christ's invitation a blessing to their souls.

TWO

What Are the Benefits of Coming to Christ?

Imagine a woman meeting a sweet guy whom she increasingly discover to be humble, modest, wise, caring, generous, self-controlled, and amusing. This man is very interested in her, and they both get on delightfully together each time they meet. Then one day he tells her he loves her, and he asks if she will become his wife. He knows that she is not all that healthy or strong, but he will look after her as a caring husband should. "Will you please do me the honor of becoming my wife?" She has been hoping for years that one day she would find such a soul mate. She chokes out a whispered yes and embraces him as her best friend, protector, lover, and husband-to-be. In the same way, coming to Christ is being joined to Him in loving matrimony.

When the King of Love, our Shepherd, invites us to come to Him and become our husband and eternal friend, He promises to come very close to us—in fact, to be in us—and never leave us, all the while giving us the most wonderful blessings. What are some of the benefits of coming to Christ?

We Are Joined to Him Forever

We have become eternally one with the loving Lord of glory. We have become partners, sharing that yoke He has made for us. We will never bear a burden alone. We are beneficiaries of His kindness, patience, wisdom, and graciousness. Everything good about us is because of Him—it's all due to His generosity. We experience the life of the Lamb of God day by day, and that is never frustrating. It is our delight. His loving holiness does not make us feel like inadequate failures. He never shames us for the inconsistency of our lives. His virtues become our template and our ambition. They inspire us to live as He lives. This divine and loving husband of ours, with whom we are eternally one, is also our enabling Lord. He is determined to gently and irresistibly transform us and give us the ability to live a new and happy life. Our lives are changed once we are joined to Him! We bear witness to His grace: "I am a different person by His enabling graciousness. He is so patient, forgiving, and encouraging. What a blessing to be joined to Him. He has given me a wholly new orientation. I am living out the righteousness that I have in the Christ I love, and my greatest desire is to reflect His beauty more and more." That is the greatest benefit of coming to Christ and being one with Him.

We Receive Rest

He says, "Come to Me, all you who labor and are heavy laden, and I will give you rest" (Matthew 11:28). These are echoes of the words of creation. After making the heavens and the earth, and creating man in His image, the Creator entered His rest. From that rest He governs a marvelous, organic machine that He designed, made, and set in motion. From His place of rest He continues working in His providence, governing all our histories. This identical rest of eternity is given by the Son of God to all His people. It has come down to earth! We enjoy this rest, no longer slaves to sin, no longer fearful of death and what lies beyond, no longer lorded over by principalities and powers and the rulers of the darkness of this world, no longer having nothing to protect us from the fiery darts of the Evil One. We rest, preserved from the fatal wounds of the flaming arrows of unbelief, alienation from God, and idolatry. We enjoy God's rest every day. Nothing can separate us from the love of God, and in that assurance we rest.

We're not uncertain about the purpose of life and what lies in our futures. We are not ignorant of our destiny, of our approaching death, and what comes afterward. We rest in peace through our Lord Jesus! By mighty Christ's omnipotence, omniscience, omnipresence, and omnicompetence, He sustains all His people, both in this world and in the world to come, with the sweetest rest. The life of heaven has begun now, and that will go on beyond the grave and will be established in the eternal rest accomplished by Christ.

Each Sunday Christians experience a foretaste of heavenly rest as we gather with others who have come to Jesus Christ. As we do so we are stating, "I don't live for my job, my business, my family, my bank balance,

for recognition, or for the glow of my own prowess. For
to me, to live is coming to Jesus Christ as my Lord and
Savior, and one whole day each week without fail I give
to Him, to learn more of Him, to find the dying embers
of my soul rekindled with new love from Him. Godly
fellowship, Christian worship, spiritual conversation,
holy meditation renews my rest every seven days. What
a refreshment from all my daily responsibilities! How
could I cope without Him, and what have I in this life
and in the world to come but Him whom my soul loves
more than anyone else?" That is the rest Jesus gives to
all who have come to Him. The weekly Sabbath rest is
our anticipation of the rest that lies before us.

We Will Never Hunger Again

The Lord Jesus said that whoever comes to Him will
never again know the pains of hunger. Imagine that for
a moment. Do you believe that extraordinary claim?
What can it mean? It means that I will always receive
from Him nourishment that satisfies my deepest longings. All people made in the image of God are restless
without Him. They will seek to appease this emptiness
by filling their hearts and souls with nonstop entertain-
ment, excitement, substances, and relationships. The
Lord Jesus clearly saw that, and He said, "You must
instead come to Me, and as you experience My goodness and grace, you will never want to seek meaning
and fulfillment in anything that's created." You have
met the Creator! What power is His who made a billion, billion galaxies! What a sense of beauty is His who

created the moon, a rainbow, a sunset, an eagle, a range of snow-covered mountains. What wisdom this preacher of the Sermon on the Mount possesses. Some people may have the ambition of actually meeting their favorite composer or author. I hope that that longing will be fulfilled for you and that the encounter will not be a disappointment, but in Jesus Christ we meet the very maker of heaven and earth! Feeding on Him will always nourish us.

Everything else is dull in comparison with Him. It lacks enduring delight, satisfaction, and joyfulness. All else is without flavor compared with what the Lord Jesus adds to every day. He satisfies our intellectual hunger as well as our aesthetic longings and desires. I enjoy the privileges of coming to Him each day, but I want more and more of Him! I want Him all! I long to be conformed to Him more and more. That is my new ambition—not temporal, tangible delights alone but the satisfaction that comes from the nearness of Jesus Christ. Nothing else can fill my hunger as He fills it. He filled a deep emptiness when I encountered Him. To have Him is everything; to want more is unnecessary. He gives forgiveness for all my misdeeds, no matter how great my shame or wayward my condition. He gives knowledge, for now I know who I am and what this life is all about. He will never fail to meet my longings, not even in eternity. He will always satisfy and enrich me. The Lord Jesus is someone I can feed and feed and feed upon.

We Will Never Be Cast Out

Again, the Lord Jesus has underlined the benefits of coming to Himself by telling the world that if they should come to Him, they will be His forever. There is no way He will ever throw out even the weakest and most backslidden Christian who has properly come to Him. However exasperating and offending Peter's conduct might have been when he repeatedly denied he had ever come to the Lord, the grieved Lord Jesus did not kick him out. Rather, He said, "Simon, Simon! Indeed, Satan has asked for you, that he may sift you as wheat. But I have prayed for you, that your faith should not fail; and when you have returned to Me, strengthen your brethren" (Luke 22:31–32). Peter did fall, but Christ kept interceding for him, whispering Peter's name in the ears of His heavenly Father, and Peter returned and mightily strengthened his brothers. He was restored. His fall was only for a season. That's why we say that those who truly come to Christ can have radical and serious falls but never totally and finally fall from grace. Their sins never provoke Jesus Christ to throw them out of the kingdom. They finally come to themselves and return to their Father. They are restored, they are humbled, they repent, and they persevere to the end, chastened with many a grievous memory. Each one who comes is saved. Not one is lost.

This perseverance does not hang on their personalities or free will; it relies wholly on God the Father giving them to His Son in love, and that love will not let them go. It is energized and perfected by Christ's purpose in coming into the world to save them from their sin. Now in heaven, He prays for them as their Great High Priest, and the Holy Spirit who indwells them makes intercession for them. The triune God will not loosen His grip on them.

Like the heroes of faith in the Old and New Testaments, believers today also fall into sin through the temptations of Satan and the influence of the world, through remaining corruption in their own hearts, and through their neglecting prayer and the privilege of walking close to the Lord. They fail to heed the warnings of the Word of God despite Jesus making spectacularly clear the perils that would face His disciples. So, down and down they fall! And they can continue in the fallenness of unbelief for a long time under the displeasure of God. They grieve His Holy Spirit, they lose their joy in knowing God, their comforts of walking with God are taken from them, their hearts are hardened, their consciences are wounded, they scandalize others and bring temporal judgments on themselves. Still, what mercy and patience God displays. There are certainly radical and serious falls, but not one is a total and final fall. Their Savior Jesus Christ will never cast them out; instead, He restores them.

What strong language Jesus uses. He does not simply say that if they come to Him, He will not cast them out. He says, "by no means" John 6:37; in other words, there is no possible way He can banish them. He has prayed, "Father, I desire that they also whom You gave Me may be with Me where I am, that they may behold My glory which You have given Me" (John 17:24). And whatever the Son of God requests, God the Father supplies. So the implications are very clear: if we continue in life with Jesus Christ, then we have indeed truly come to Him. If we fall away and never return, then we never really came to Him at all. This is what the apostle John says of those who left the company of the disciples: "They went out from us, but they were not of us; for if they had been of us, they would have continued with us; but they went out that they might be made manifest, that none of them were of us" (1 John 2:19). They had never truly come to Jesus Christ in a way the Scripture describes as the God-honoring, effectual way.

We love to affirm in our doxology those beautiful words of Augustus Toplady,

> Yes, I to the end shall endure
> As sure as the earnest is given.
> More happy but not more secure
> The glorified spirits in heaven

Perseverance encourages praise. The whole process by which we are kept in a state of grace is a divine accomplishment. If I start to become confident that my preservation is due to my constantly making the right choice of deciding for Jesus, then I am patting myself on the back. But if my hope rests in the power of Christ to sustain me with His grace and by the power of His intercession, then I am going to praise Him as night approaches that He has brought me a day's march nearer home.

Hence, this status of being accepted by Jesus Christ is fixed forever. There is no way you can slip out of it. There is no way the devil can overcome you and take you to hell. You are heaven-bound! Do you see what that means for your whole future? This is your certain and sure hope, and so you live accordingly. "For to me, to live is Christ," you say to yourself. You put to death remaining sin's deceits and seek a closer walk with Jesus. We pay heed to God's law—its teaching, correction, reproofs, and training in righteousness.

We Will Be Raised Up on the Last Day

Being "raised up on the last day" is a startling claim recorded by John in what is considered to be the oldest and most profound of the Gospels. The shock of this claim may not be immediately evident. We have been thinking about the simple theme of coming to Christ and the benefits that this coming to Him will bring to us, but now these words lift us into the huge world of Christian supernaturalism—of the end of the world, death, resurrection, the day of judgment, and the eternal state. There is no way such words of Jesus can be brushed aside. Christianity claims that what we sow will we also reap, and that we face a day of accountability for our lives—lives that have been sustained by God. Our breath and heartbeat are all in God's hands. We are being kept by His power until our death—and after that, the judgment. Who is going to judge us? Yes, it is Jesus of Nazareth, the Son of God. Such a claim is either the rambling words of a megalomaniac or the words of God our Creator.

It is possible to think very sweetly about coming to the Lord Jesus and becoming His disciples. The wise of the world will nod their heads and consider that a person's whole life might be quite enriched by the influence of the New Testament. Living one's life by following the example of the teacher of the Sermon on the Mount suggests the possibility of someone attaining a certain nobility, an ethical attractiveness. But in this claim of Jesus Christ to raise us from the dead, we are confronted with an opinion that utterly contradicts the common idea of the twenty-first century that death is annihilation followed by nothingness. There will be resurrection and judgment, with our Lord deciding our eternal destinies. There is scarcely anything more alien to the ethos of the modern world's thinking than these words of His: "No one can come to Me unless the Father who sent Me draws him; and I will raise him up at the last day" (John 6:44).

The Lord Jesus says the only possible way for us to come to Him is by God the Father determining to home in on us, changing our hearts and drawing us to follow His Son. Without that we shall remain without Christ. I encourage you to start thinking about all you are learning in this book, speaking to God and asking for His grace and mercy, that He should draw you to Christ.

When the Apostles' Creed is repeated week by week in churches all over the world, the congregation says together, "We believe in the resurrection of the dead."

Why do they declare this? Because the Bible loudly and clearly tells us so. We are told that all who come to Christ will be raised from the dead to eternal glory. There is going to be an extraordinary climax in the future, a day when Jesus—the conqueror of death who rose on the third day, who raised several people from the dead, who spoke and the winds and waves obeyed Him—will raise the dead back to life. Our bodies are going to die, but our souls never die. The body temporarily ceases to function, but not the inner person. Physical death does not end our lives, just one segment of our lives; it is one step in the ongoing process of conscious life. Death tears apart body and soul, but the dead shall live again. The Son of God is going to raise them up.

The Old Testament speaks explicitly about a future resurrection for all who have died. Hannah, the mother of Samuel, said, "The LORD kills and makes alive; He brings down to the grave and brings up" (1 Samuel 2:6). The patriarch Job, after suffering much anguish, said, "For I know that my Redeemer lives, and He shall stand at last on the earth; and after my skin is destroyed, this I know, that in my flesh I shall see God" (Job 19:25–26). Job knew his body would be destroyed, but he also had the promise that God would raise him again someday, body and soul. Job had the belief in a personal resurrection. The psalmist wrote, "Therefore my heart is glad, and my glory rejoices; my flesh also will rest in hope. For You will not leave my soul in Sheol, nor will You allow Your Holy One to see corruption" (Psalm 16:9–10).

Another psalmist was inspired to write, "As for me, I will see Your face in righteousness; I shall be satisfied when I awake in Your likeness" (Psalm 17:15).

The prophets Elijah and Elisha were both used by God to raise children from the dead. The prophet Daniel realized there was hope of a resurrection beyond the grave, writing, "And many of those who sleep in the dust of the earth shall awake, some to everlasting life, some to shame and everlasting contempt" (Daniel 12:2). God speaking through the prophet Isaiah said, "Your dead shall live; together with my dead body they shall arise. Awake and sing, you who dwell in dust; for your dew is like the dew of herbs, and the earth shall cast out the dead" (Isaiah 26:19). And speaking through Hosea He says, "I will ransom them from the power of the grave; I will redeem them from death. O Death, I will be your plagues! O Grave, I will be your destruction" (Hosea 13:14).

Thus we find the hope of the resurrection being announced and the power to raise the dead displayed in the Old Testament. The teaching of Christ concerning a future day of resurrection was simply a repetition and enrichment of the Scriptures' teaching on this subject. Jesus said, "For as the Father raises the dead and gives life to them, even so the Son gives life to whom He will" (John 5:21). He also said, "Do not marvel at this; for the hour is coming in which all who are in the graves will hear His voice and come forth—those who have done good, to the resurrection of life, and those who have done evil, to the resurrection of condemnation" (John 5:28–29). And again, "This is the will of the Father who sent Me, that of all He has given Me I should lose nothing, but should raise it up at the last day" (John 6:39). Jesus also said, "I am the resurrection and the life. He who believes in Me, though he may die, he shall live" (John 11:25).

Teaching on the resurrection of believers was a part of the early preaching of the apostles, who had spent three years in the presence of Christ. We are told of His enemies that they were "greatly disturbed" because the apostles "taught the people and preached in Jesus the resurrection from the dead" (Acts 4:2). When the apostle Paul was speaking in Athens to the Greek philosophers, we are told, "Certain Epicurean and Stoic philosophers encountered him. And some said, 'What does this babbler want to say?' Others said, 'He seems to be a proclaimer of foreign gods,' because he preached to them Jesus and the resurrection…. [Paul said,] 'He has appointed a day on which He will judge the world in righteousness by the Man whom He has ordained. He has given assurance of this to all by raising Him from the dead'" (Acts 17:18, 31).

There are rich passages in the letters that Paul wrote in which he gives special attention to the subject of the resurrection. In a long chapter in his first letter to the Corinthians (chapter 15), Paul states that Christ's own resurrection guarantees ours. We will have a body that will be related to our former body but also be like the one possessed by the resurrected Christ. In his second letter to the Corinthians, Paul also says, "For we know that if our earthly house, this tent, is destroyed, we have a building from God, a house not made with hands, eternal in the heavens. For in this we groan, earnestly desiring to be clothed with our habitation which is from heaven, if indeed, having been clothed, we shall not be found naked. For we who are in this tent groan, being burdened, not because we want to be unclothed, but further clothed, that mortality may be swallowed up by life" (2 Corinthians 5:1–4). Finally, in the first letter to the Thessalonians he speaks of the certainty of the resurrection:

> But I do not want you to be ignorant, brethren, concerning those who have fallen asleep, lest you sorrow as others who have no hope. For if we believe that Jesus died and rose again, even so God will bring with Him those who sleep in Jesus.
>
> For this we say to you by the word of the Lord, that we who are alive and remain until the coming of the Lord will by no means precede those who are asleep. For the Lord Himself will descend from heaven with a shout, with the voice of an archangel, and with the trumpet of God. And the dead in Christ will rise first. Then we who are alive and remain shall be caught up together with them in the clouds to meet the Lord in the air. And thus we shall always be with the Lord. Therefore comfort one another with these words. (1 Thessalonians 4:13–18)

But it is the Lord Jesus who is the first to have been raised from the dead, never to die again. His resurrection was unique. Others whom the Bible records as being raised from the dead eventually died again. Jesus rose to die no more. He said, "I am He who lives, and was dead, and behold, I am alive forevermore" (Revelation 1:18), and His apostle Paul affirms that Christ was the first to rise from the dead in a new body: "Therefore, having obtained help from God, to this day I stand, witnessing both to small and great, saying no other things than those which the prophets and Moses said would come—that the Christ would suffer, that He would be the first to rise from the dead" (Acts 26:22–23).

So we cannot separate the essential need for us to come to Jesus Christ from the reality of who the Bible declares this person to be—God incarnate, whom one day all men are going to meet, before whom every knee will bow. The Lord Christ Himself will raise the dead, and this resurrection will be universal. There will then be a bifurcation of human destinies: a resurrection unto life and a resurrection unto death, or separation from God. Those who are raised will never die again. The resurrection will be a prelude to the final judgment of both the righteous and the wicked. Can't you see how coming to Christ is a matter of eternal importance, of vindication in the great day of judgment or of separation from God?

THREE

What Are the Warnings for Failing to Come?

There is no way we would want to avoid warnings of danger ahead: Bridge Closed. Adult Content. Dead End. Do Not Enter. Do Not Approach the Buffalo. Poison. No Jumping Off Bridge. High Voltage. Stop. Wrong Way. The highway code will explain to us many useful symbols of potential danger on roads. Parents will warn their children about touching electrical sockets and the danger of crossing a road without looking both ways. In the countryside farmers will warn city dwellers of dangers from herds of cattle or from paddling in rivers.

There are warnings built into all the teachings of the Lord Jesus Christ. His ministry was not that of an enigmatic guru, sitting with a half smile, saying that all was well. This is a groaning world where men do unthinkable things to other men, to women, and even to children. What cruelty animals face in their brief lives. God does not shrug! The Lord Jesus spoke of a God who is light, a righteous and holy Father, a consuming fire, who hates cruelty, torture, and abuse.

Many Christian people have heard of an Australian named Arthur Malcolm Stace (February 9, 1885–July 30, 1967), known as "Mr. Eternity." He was born in New South Wales near Sydney in 1885. His parents were alcoholics, and he was raised in poverty. In order to survive, he resorted to stealing bread and milk and searching for scraps of food in garbage cans. By the age of twelve, Stace, with virtually no formal schooling and working in a coal mine, had become a ward of the state. At fifteen he was an alcoholic and was subsequently sent to jail. In his twenties he was a scout for his sisters' brothels. You would consider there to be little hope for such a man. He seems destined to be another statistic of ruined and self-destroyed men.

On August 6, 1930, Stace was taken to church at forty-five years of age. He came to Christ under the preaching of R. B. S. Hammond, and his whole life went in a new direction. Two years later he heard John G. Ridley speaking on Isaiah 57:15: "For thus says the High and Lofty One who inhabits eternity, whose name is Holy: 'I dwell in the high and holy place, with him who has a contrite and humble spirit, to revive the spirit of the humble, and to revive the heart of the contrite ones.'"

Arthur Stace was overwhelmed with the thought of the high and lofty One that inhabits eternity as John Ridley cried, "Eternity! Eternity! I wish that I could sound that word to everyone on the streets of Sydney. We all have to meet God. Where will you spend eternity?" Arthur said, "Eternity rang through my brain and I began to weep. Increasingly I felt a powerful

conviction that I should write down the word Eternity."
He was illiterate; he could hardly write his own name
legibly, yet when he kneeled down and wrote the word
eternity on the sidewalk, it came out smoothly in a beautiful copperplate script. "I couldn't understand it. I still
can't," he said.[1]

So the pattern of his weeks began. Several mornings
a week for the next thirty-five years, Stace left his wife,
Pearl, around 5 a.m. to go around the streets of Sydney
and chalk this word of warning, *eternity*, on footpaths,
railway station entrances, and anywhere else he thought
suitable. It is estimated that he wrote this word of warning around five hundred thousand times over those
years. Workers arriving in the city would see the word
freshly written but not who wrote it. So "The Man Who
Writes Eternity" became a legend in Sydney. He died
in 1967 at age eighty-two. On December 31, 1999, one
of the first places on earth to welcome the new millen-
nium was Australia, and the Sydney Harbour Bridge
was lit up with fireworks. Suddenly the word *eternity*
in the unmistakable copperplate writing of Arthur Stace
was writ large over the side of the bridge to be seen and
read on television all over the world.

That one word is itself a warning. Consider your
choices in light of eternity. In all of Christ's invitations
there are inbuilt warnings about the consequences of
not coming. In John's gospel these words of the Lord

1. See Roy Williams and Elizabeth Meyers, *Mr. Eternity: The
Story of Arthur Stace* (Sydney: Acorn Press, 2017).

Jesus are recorded: "But you are not willing to come to Me that you may have life" (John 5:40). Some men sat with five thousand others and heard Him preach as no other person had ever preached. They ate from the five loaves and two fishes that He had multiplied to satisfy the hunger of them all. Yet most of them likely muttered as they walked away, "That fellow could make you believe that black was white." They had tasted and profited from the miracle of His feeding, all of them had eaten from a mere five loaves and two fishes, but they devised some far-fetched explanation of that too. Others saw Him raise Lazarus from the tomb and subsequently spoke to Lazarus about it, but they said, "Of course he never had died. He was resting in the tomb recuperating for a few days." They all shrugged and looked for other explanations for being affected by Jesus's life and words and work. But the truth was devastating: they were forfeiting eternal life by choosing to reject Him.

Let me appeal to your own self-interest. Wouldn't it be better for you to be reconciled to the God of heaven than to be His enemy? What are you getting by opposing your God? Are you the happier for being His enemy? You whose life revolves around the pub, have you found meaning and love in a pint? Let your conscience speak and answer whether you have found your rest and peace by your own behavior. I exhort you by everything that is sacred, everything that is important and eternal: flee for your lives to Christ, and don't look back. Do not stay where you are any longer until you have found cleansing for your guilt and also knowledge of who God is in the Lord Jesus Christ.

Do you know what it is you are rejecting? You are rejecting Jesus Christ our Creator, the Son of God, the only Savior, aren't you? I cannot bear that you should do this, for I remember what you are forgetting: the day is coming when you will want a Savior. It is not long before weary months will have ended and your strength begins to decline; your heartbeat will become irregular, you will become weak and need help to stand and take a single step. You and the grim monster, death, must face each other. What will you do then without a Savior? Deathbeds are stony places on which to lie without the Lord Jesus Christ. It's an awful thing to die anyhow. A man with the purest life and strongest hope in Jesus finds that death is not a thing to take lightly. It is a fearful thing to pass from the seen to the unseen, from the mortal to the immortal, from time to eternity, and you are going to take that journey alone? David said that though he journeyed through the valley of the shadow of death he would fear no evil, for the Lord and His comfort would be with him. It will be a hard thing to die without Christ. I cannot help thinking of you dying without hope. I cannot bear that. I imagine standing by your coffin, looking into your cold face, and saying, "This man would not come to Christ for life. He neglected the great salvation."

But let this message enter your heart for another reason. I picture myself standing at the bar of God. As the Lord lives, the day of judgment is coming. Do you believe that? The poisoner and the rapist and the torturer and the mass killer, the maker of concentration camps and the pits full of bodies—don't you think that one day the sin of the men who did that will find them out? There is a coming day when God shall judge the world in righteousness. And you? The eye of God is fixed on you. It seems to you that He is not looking anywhere else, but only on you, and He summons you before Him. He reads your sins; how will He evaluate your life? "You would not come to Me for mercy when it was offered to you. Have things changed since then? Do I see a heart of love and repentance now when you see Me face to face? No! Then depart from Me. I now have ceased inviting unbelievers to come from their rejection of Me to trust in Me. Go from My presence."

Oh, my friend, I cannot let you refuse to come to Jesus Christ without a word. If I should see a man acting suspiciously on the platform as a train comes racing in, I would have to say to him, "Hello, friend! Are you OK? Can I help you?" I should be destitute of all humanity if I remained silent. And I should be worse than a fiend if I didn't now, with love and kindness and earnestness, beseech you to come to the loving Son of God. Consider the warnings of gentle Jesus, meek and mild, so patient and pure.

It is frightening but true that when the Lord Jesus promises He will not cast out those who do come, He is also inferring that all who refuse will indeed be cast out. If He promises rest to all who come, He is inferring there will be no rest for those who defy His invitation.

If those who come to Christ will never again be hungry, then those who contemptuously turn away from Him will never stop being famished; even after death there will be gnashing of teeth.

So you see that this subject of coming to the inviting Jesus Christ is of the utmost importance to everyone reading these words. This is not a mere theological or methodological study. Coming to Christ is a matter of being given the rest of Jesus or being denied that blessed rest. Coming to Christ is a matter of being satisfied with Him or being indifferent. Coming to Christ is a matter of being received into His love or being cast away from Him, of being raised up at the last day justified or being raised up to be condemned. Coming to Christ is not a matter of scoring theological points. It is not a matter of titillating our intellects. It is life or death. How crucial this matter is!

But I must continue in explaining to you what coming to Christ entails, and it is important that we clear away the rubble that hides the true meaning of this action.

FOUR

A True Coming Is Not a Physical Action

When Jesus said, "Come to Me…and I will give you rest," He was not talking about some sort of overt physical act. Yet a lot of professing Christians equate coming to Christ with this very thing. Let me explain what I mean. Imagine that an evangelist has just finished preaching, opening up the Scriptures. He has shown the plight of man and the power of God. He has explained the cross on which the Prince of Glory died, and now he is engaging with his congregation. He lays the claims of Christ on them—pleading, urging them to repent and believe. "Cry mightily to God! Bow before Him! Receive Him into your hearts." He doesn't stop. He is near tears and beseeches them not to tarry. "If not now, then when?" He is longing for a response. He is not satisfied in giving them a glorified Bible study, correctly exegeting a passage of the Scriptures and then saying "Amen." He is an ambassador and herald of the King of Heaven, preaching for a response. He is doing the work of an evangelist. He is like John Knox, who seemed to beat the pulpit into pieces in his enthusiasm for people to turn from unbelief to trusting in and obeying the Lord. The Christian congregation is drawn into this engagement. He speaks on behalf of them all. And he cries aloud on their behalf to the Holy Spirit to help him, "Come now Spirit of God, come now and assist us. Come and draw sinners to Jesus!" He is a true preacher, and we thank God for him.

We see that illustrated in one of the great evangelists of the past, George Whitefield, when he went to Cambuslang, Scotland, in 1742. He preached on Isaiah 54:5, "Your Maker is your husband," and coming to the climax of his sermon, he addressed the congregation, challenging them, "Are any of you prepared to take Christ for your husband?" He showed them their need and how Christ met it. Whitefield urged them to close with Him by entrusting themselves to Him that night. "Come, and I will marry you to him just now." A twenty-one-year-old man was one of those whose heart was opened. He told his friends later that when Whitefield "laid out the terms" of union with Christ, he found his "heart making sweet agreement to those terms." Another convert later hugged a friend, exclaiming that the minister had "married my soul to Christ." Whitefield wrote that many "were married to the Lord Jesus that night."

When the preacher explains the gospel; magnifies Christ in the glory of His person and the perfection of His finished work as our prophet, priest, and king; and speaks of His readiness to receive any who will call on His name and then urges them to do so, then he is displaying the wholeness of New Testament evangelism. But many go further than that. They break through boundaries that God has laid down. They intrude into the work of the Holy Spirit, and that is an honor He refuses to give to any man.

A friend of mine, Elly Achok Olare, is a minister in Kenya whom I taught in the Trinity Reformed Baptist seminary in Nairobi. For many years before he understood the Bible properly, he had been linked with a group of churches that used human psychology to manufacture a physical outward response to the claims of Christ over men's lives. He describes the techniques he saw employed and, sadly, had been taught to use: They would print posters to advertise the coming evangelistic meetings and the miracles that would occur. There would be an image of the preacher and pictures of discarded crutches and empty wheelchairs. A band would be brought in to entice those who would not be interested in listening to a preacher. Then church members were taught how they were to act that evening. If the evangelist asked for a show of hands for those who had become Christians, they were to raise their hands to encourage others to do the same. It is a display of the herding instinct! Then when a so-called altar call took place and people were urged to get out of their seats and walk to the front, the Christians were told that they were to be the first on their feet to come to stand before the stage. Elly describes it like this:

> It is much like the animal world—such as the great wildebeest migration across the Mara river

in Kenya. There is nervous reluctance, the herds stand on the bank knowing of the crocodiles in the river, but when finally one wildebeest makes the jump the rest follow suit at the exact spot where the first one crossed the river. This is the psychology employed to get the timid masses to come forward and "receive Jesus."…

Most crusades are timed to end as the sun sets. This is to take advantage of the cover of darkness so that the people who feel like getting up and going to the front may not feel embarrassed, since no one is seeing them. Over and above that but even during day time such psychological tactics like saying, "everybody close your eyes" will be used in the service. This is to ensure that those being urged to come forward may feel that no one is looking at them. The first step having been secured with every eye closed (probably under cover of darkness) the second step is put into place. With a sombre and emotional voice carried melodiously over the notes of soft music, the preacher asks those who want to make a commitment to Jesus to lift up their hands. There will follow a protracted encouragement, prodding and appealing to them all not to be ashamed of the Lord. Then closed eyes will be urged upon everyone. ("You need not worry, no one is watching you.")[1]

Preachers who use such tactics are not showing confidence in God. They are simply employing human engineering. If there are not enough responses to the altar call, the evangelist's tone might change and he will

---

1. Elly Achok Olare, *Hell's Best Revealed Secret* (Mumias, Kenya: Gospel Missions Agency Church, 2014), 2–3.

start to cajole the people to get up and walk to the front. He tries to bring all kinds of pressure to bear on them, charging them with cowardice, urging them not to be ashamed of "taking their stand" for Christianity. "Come to the front" is his refrain, his mission, and the focus of his exhortation. That movement is being equated—both in the understanding of the preacher and increasingly by everyone else—with the spiritual act of coming to the Son of God. What ungodly confusion!

The preacher announces that all who have gotten out of their seats and responded to his invitation have also responded to the Lord Jesus's invitation to come to Him. He might keep a book called the "Lamb's Book of Life," where he records the names of people who have come to the front over the years. But no one in the church has ever heard of those people. This plea for an overt physical response to an altar call has become so common in certain circles that wherever it happens, people are convinced there has also been the inward spiritual reality of coming to Christ.

Of course, I am not denying that we are to preach for the obedience of faith, that people are not to hesitate in coming to Jesus Christ as they hear the gospel. One does not question the fact that people are converted in meetings at which they hear the gospel of God loving the world and giving His only Son. We do not question the sincerity or motives of such men as Billy Graham, George Beverly Shea, and Cliff Barrows. But no one was ever saved by walking from point A to point B. No one has ever been saved by standing, or raising a hand, or any kind of overt physical act. Some are converted during those types of meetings, but it is in spite of the tactics, not because of them. It is because the gospel of Jesus Christ was preached.

Hear what the Lord Jesus says in John 6:44: "No one can come to Me unless the Father who sent Me draws him." If coming to Christ is some kind of human action, then I don't need a special inward operation of the Holy Spirit, which Jesus defines as a "drawing of the Father," to do that. All I need is a burst of courage to get up and walk to the front. I don't need the drawing of the Father to do that. But the Bible teaches that no man can come to Christ repenting of sin and trusting in Him unless there is an inward divine operation of God.

Dr. Martyn Lloyd-Jones, in the final chapter of his riveting book on preaching titled *Preaching and Preachers*, expresses at length his unhappiness with the so-called altar call. In his opinion, the most serious issue is the organizers' and preacher's misunderstanding of the doctrine of regeneration: "This action of coming to Jesus Christ is the work of the Holy Spirit, and his work alone, no one else can do it. The true work of conviction of sin, and regeneration, and the giving of the gift of faith and new life is solely the work of the Holy Spirit. And as it is his work it is always a thorough work; and it is always a work that will show itself."[2] As an illustration of this, Lloyd-Jones refers to Peter's sermon in Acts 2

---

2. David Martyn Lloyd-Jones, *Preaching and Preachers* (London: Hodder and Stoughton, 1971), 291.

and how his hearers cried out under the conviction of sin that came from hearing what Peter had said, "Brethren, what shall we do?" (Acts 2:37). They didn't wait for an invitation to respond, and no music was needed to set the mood; the Spirit did the work.

If any of you reading these words is certain you've come to Christ simply because you once passed through some outward physical action, then I trust that the Spirit of God will utterly strip this false notion from you today. May God use His Word as a purging influence so that you will never think, let alone speak, in terms of equating a physical action with the inward reality of the act of coming to Christ.

What of the fruit of this method of evangelism? There is a pervasive questioning in the professing church today of the invitation system's methodology. Consider the following statistics. In November of 1970, a number of churches in Fort Worth, Texas, secured thirty thousand decisions for Christ. Six months later, the follow-up committee only found thirty who still held to any form of the Christian faith. In September of 1977, *Eternity Magazine* gave the results of an evangelistic crusade in which the invitation system was employed. They found that 4,106 attendees claimed to have made a decision for Jesus Christ. Shortly afterward, several churches who sponsored the event followed up with the people who made those claims and found that only 125 of them had joined a local church. The rest could not be accounted for. To do the mathematics, out of 4,106 decisions for Christ, 3,981 of them were not bearing any biblical fruit that the churches could discern. That means only 3 percent of the new converts were actually living like new converts.

The problem is this: when you try to replace a work of God with a work of man, you will always fail. History has proven that time and time again. Man cannot by himself come to Christ. Man cannot create a new creation. Man cannot raise a dead sinner from the grave. Man cannot give himself a heart of flesh. Only God can do that. Only His methods work. Preaching the gospel and pleading with sinners are the means that God has appointed to bring about conversion. Any addition or deviation from that is an attempt to manufacture conversions with the methods of men, not God.

When an evangelist's mindset is that someone has come to Christ because they got out of their seat and walked forward, there's going to be a fallout. When a message is presented, intentionally or unintentionally, that salvation can be attained by physical actions, there will be death, not life. People will think they are converted when they are not. They will soon be disappointed that they feel the same as they did a week or month earlier. They will become increasingly aware that there is no inward change. When repentance and faith are ignored but salvation is assumed, problems are sure to come.

FIVE

A True Coming Is Not a Purely Intellectual Act

When Jesus said, "Come to Me...and I will give you rest," He was not talking about a merely mental act. Again, many are deceived on this point. They attend a series of classes introducing the Christian religion. They are told that God is their Maker and that Jesus Christ is His Son. They are taught that He lived a sinless life and died for sinners, that He rose again the third day and is seated at the right hand of God, and that forgiveness of sins is found in Him. These propositions are laid out before the class. "Now," the class is finally asked, "do you believe these things to be true?" The students think for a moment, and then most of them nod and one by one say, "Yeah..." Then they are told that that means they are now Christians.

The students have been told that the essence of coming to Christ is assenting to the facts about Him. Then, by nodding their heads to a brief systematic presentation of Christianity, they are assured they have actually now come to Christ. They are given this assurance, personally and solemnly by the person leading the course, that they are now Christians. In other words, another human being gives them assurance that all is well between them and God. That human being seems to be the most religious person they have ever met. If anyone should know who a Christian is, then it is bound to be him, and so, though they don't feel much different from how they were before beginning the course, they have now set into this new status of being a "real Christian."

Again, I submit to you that if this is true, then John 6:44 had better be cut out of our Bibles. It states in simple language that "no one can come to Me unless the Father who sent Me draws him." Who needs the Holy Spirit to assent to historical facts about the gospel? Just as the average man needs no work or operation of the Holy Spirit on his heart and mind to accept that in 1492 Columbus sailed the ocean blue, so too men and women can exercise some mental activity about the Jesus of history—His virgin birth, death on the cross, and resurrection on the third day. They may believe those things to be true, but such a "faith" is not coming to Christ. That is not saving faith; that is believing the system of Christian teaching. James tells us that the devils believe these facts about God are true—that He is triune, holy, a judge, and has sent His Son to be the Savior of the world. The devils believe all that. They know the contents of the Bible and can quote them.

One of the main differences between the first-century church and our modern church is that those people knew God intimately. They had a relationship with the Lord that wasn't waiting to start in heaven; it was working in them while they were still in this world. They didn't have the advantages of radio, television, internet, or any other modern means of communication. There was nothing like an equivalent to our bumper stickers to put on their chariots. Yet these believers turned the known world upside down with the truths of the gospel, their communion with God, their earnest testimony of what the Lord Jesus had done, their corporate character in peace and godliness when they met together, and their righteous personal lives (Acts 17:6). They impacted their world much more than we are impacting our world today. Why?

They had such a depth of relationship with a living God that it was contagious. People took note that they had been with Jesus. In Rome, Christians knew their God so intimately that they sang His praises as they were burned at the stake. There are historical accounts of Nero the emperor sticking his fingers in his ears and saying, "Why must these Christians sing?"

They had much more than a doctrine. They had a present-tense relationship that allowed them to endure terrible atrocities with joy. There are historical accounts of Romans, when witnessing the joy of these Christians who were being martyred, jumping out of the stands and rushing to them. They knew they would be doomed to the same fate, but they willingly accepted death so they could know God in the same close, intimate, and personal way as these Christians.

Let me ask you this question. It's intended not to condemn you but to enlighten you. How many people would die to have what you have? Is anyone envious of your relationship with the Lord? If not, then I suggest you aren't experiencing eternal life as the Bible describes it and as our Lord Jesus died to give you.

This isn't something for the select few. This is normal Christian living. In fact, if this isn't your experience, you aren't really living. This is what drove the apostle Paul (Philippians 3:10) and all the early Christians. It's still what drives victorious Christians today. It's not just mental assent to a doctrine; it is all about personal relationship with the living God.

SIX

A True Coming Is Not a Mystical Experience Ungrounded in the Bible

When the Lord Jesus said, "Come to Me...and I will give you rest," He was not talking about a mystical experience ungrounded in the truth. Many churchgoers have a vague belief and have made a vague commitment to a Christ whom they vaguely know. Many people claim to believe in God like that. That is not coming to Christ. Our Lord Jesus Christ once addressed the people listening to Him and told them, "You do not have [God's] word abiding in you" (John 5:38). How could He make that judgment? He explained to them that they were rejecting the very One whom God had sent into the world (that is, Himself). He alone was the transcript of God's glory and the express image of God's person. If someone had seen the Lord Jesus Christ, they were in fact looking at God, for He and God are one. Jesus's words and actions are the only means of knowing in any detail and with any certainty who and what God is.

So what are people to do? Jesus tells them, "Search the Scriptures, for in them you think you have eternal life; and these are they which testify of Me" (John 5:39).

Who is Jesus? What kind of nature does He have? Was He sent on a mission? By whom? What has He done? Why did He do it? What are the implications for me? What must I do to be saved? What does a Christian believe? What is coming to Christ? How does a Christian live? What lies after death? The Scriptures give me the answers. Eternal life is all bound up in them. A man who is a stranger to the Scriptures is a stranger to eternal life because the Scriptures bear witness to the Son of God. If you want to find Jesus and come to Him, you must know the message of the Bible. It is impossible to find Him if we ignore the Scriptures. He is not a vague, undefined Christ. He is not one who changes from century to century, or from one individual to another, or from one culture to another. He is the unchangeable Christ of the Bible. There is no white Christ or black Christ or yellow Christ. There is no feminist Christ or socialist Christ or capitalist Christ. There is the one and only Lord Jesus Christ.

In Paul's letters to Timothy, the apostle exhorts him to preach the Word. He reminds him that all Scripture is God-breathed and that it is very profitable for teaching us what we are to believe—rebuking us when we imbibe error, correcting our prejudices, and instructing us in living righteously. All the time we are to be changing our values and behavior in light of the Bible, sorting out our thinking by way of the Scriptures. That is the way we are taught by God; that is the way we are drawn to Jesus Christ. So coming to Christ involves three things: the Scriptures, their testimony concerning the person and work of the Lord Jesus Christ, and our understanding and believing that testimony as it is recorded in the pages of God's divine Word. So unless I have some understanding of the Christ of the Scriptures, I have little understanding of obeying His invitation to come.

Aren't there people today who lack a basic grasp of who Jesus is—His preexistence, His perfection, His teaching, His atonement, His present reign and influence? They have some sort of mawkish and cloying religion with a vague idea or ideal that they call "Jesus." Have such people truly come to the Christ of the Bible? According to Jesus, coming to Him is a response to learning about Him from what men who wrote the Scriptures had received from God Himself. So coming to Christ is not a mystical, private experience unfounded in the truth. If I said to you, "I think of Jesus like this…" then those ideas would be worthless if I had not received them exactly from the Word of God.

There is a school of theology called neoorthodoxy, which promotes the claim that by itself the Bible is unreliable. Scripture is said to be a mixture of truth and error, and each person has to decide for himself what to receive and what to reject. But it is not important, these theologians add, that the Scriptures are wholly accurate. There can be errors in the Bible, but that is insignificant as long as the big, dynamic, mysterious Word itself zaps you. Questions of whether Jesus literally walked on water, smote a fig tree, and fed five thousand men with five loaves and two fishes are not important. What actually occurred when He hung on the cross is open to discussion and to various interpretations. Who this Jesus is—as far as defining Him theologically—is for students of historical theology to debate. All we need to do is find some religious experience, some common denominator, and say to the unbelieving world that "Jesus," whom we cannot explain without references to the Scriptures, "is alive today" in a way no one can define lucidly. Isn't it the thought of Jesus, and the ideal of Jesus, and your own private and precious concept of some kind of Jesus that is the key? No, it is not! That kind of thought is merely an expression of the religious sentimentality that has no more power to justify me and bring me into a secure relationship of a pardoned sinner before God than the lyrics of "Kumbaya." My acceptance with God hangs on my acceptance of who that Jesus Christ is and what that Jesus Christ has said and done as it is recorded in the Scriptures.

The four gospel writers tell us in exhaustive detail who Jesus of Nazareth is, what He did, when He did it, why He did it, and what He has given us to believe. That is the message of what we call the Great Commission. "You tell them all I have told you," He said. Jesus said that if we were embarrassed by His words, then He would be ashamed of us in the day of judgment. Paul says that if Jesus Christ was not physically raised from the dead, then we are still in our sins and our faith is in vain. We insist that coming to Christ is not a purely mystical experience unrelated to what God has revealed of Him in the Bible.

So coming to Christ is not a physical action like moving across a room or kneeling down or raising a hand. It is not a purely mental action of asserting some facts about Christ. It is not a mystical, private, secret action hidden away in your own soul unrelated to the truth of God in the Bible. But there is one more thing that coming to Christ is not.

SEVEN

A True Coming Does Not Separate Salvation from Submission

Coming to Christ is the response of obedience to His invitation. We are able to come to Him because He invites us and enables us by His Spirit to do so. We come to Him and stop right there, in His presence. That is crucial. We do not come to Him on our way to something more important, to the things that really matter in our lives—a person, a business, a life of partying and fun. Jesus Christ says, "Come to Me," and we come to Him alone and stay there. We listen to what He has to say. We come to Him for the first, conscious, definitive, life-changing time, and then we continue coming to Him for the rest of our lives.

Yet Christians will interpret their pilgrimage in different ways. They might have been told that God will allow them to receive all the benefits of the salvation of Jesus Christ: the full forgiveness of all their sins, past, present, and future; the certainty that they will go to heaven when they die; all the blessings of Christ as their teacher and shepherd. "These are now all yours!"

But then, they have been taught, there will come a big step in their lives when they take on board the lordship of Christ over their lives and they become more serious and consecrated disciples. They have now "laid all on the altar."

So they have been taught that before that time they may see themselves as being converted but not as being consecrated. They have taken Jesus as their Savior and received all the benefits of His salvation but still continued to behave as someone who loved the world. It was inferred that this was a perfectly normal Christian life. Then one day they were convicted of the hypocrisy and disobedience of this lifestyle, and from that time onward they not only had Christ as Savior but obeyed Him as Lord. They began to attend church again, to pray, to guard their tongues, and so on. That such experiences take place in the lives of some who come to Christ cannot be denied, but are they giving their experiences the right interpretation?

A. W. Tozer recalls a ministers' fraternal in which he and a group of preachers were having a meal in a restaurant together between the morning and afternoon sessions. One of the preachers was saying to them how easy it was to make a person a Christian. "I will show you," he said, speaking into their raised eyebrows and shaking heads of opposition to his words. The next time the waiter came over, he spoke to him. "Wouldn't you like to know the goodness of God in your life and receive Jesus as your Lord and Savior and have all your sins forgiven?" The man hesitated for a moment and

then said "Well, yes." "Then will you repeat these words
after me?" "OK," said the man, and he did repeat these
words: "Lord, I receive you into my heart as my God
and Savior, in Jesus's name, amen." He shook the man
by the hand, sat down, turned to the listening preachers,
and said, "See!" The waiter had repeated a brief sentence, the meaning of its words he barely understood, if
at all. You could hardly say that he had made any decision, or that he had come to believe on the Lord Jesus
Christ, or that all the benefits of Christ henceforth were
now his. He had repeated a sentence—maybe in hope
of a larger tip—and been given a false assurance that he
now knew God.

Dr. John Piper is most helpful in describing how he
responds to those who claim they have Christ as Savior
but not as their Lord. He remembers a converted Catho-
lic monk who professed conversion in an experience he
had during evening prayers in the monastery. He later
left the monastery and spoke in different churches. He
described his Christian life in two stages: first as Savior
and then submitting to him as Lord. He worshiped with
John Piper and joined the family for Sunday lunch, and
John Piper was unhappy with his self-assessment. He
said to him,

> "You know, Bill (not his real name), I think Jesus
> was your Lord before that later act of submission.
> I think he was your Lord the night you were con-
> verted and since then your experience has been
> one of more and more yieldedness to his sovereign
> rights as Lord over your life. And I don't think that

you have bowed to his lordship consistently since that time you 'made him Lord.' You are not fully yielded now or you would be sinless. But he is still your Lord now. And you were not fully yielded then, but he was your Lord then."

Bill was stunned. No one had ever challenged his interpretation of his Christian pilgrimage before this time. After a few minutes he turned to John and said, "You know, I think you're right." He had never been at ease in describing his life by that familiar but erroneous paradigm and was glad to think of it in a wiser, more pastoral way.

Piper continues,

> From the time of our first saving acceptance of Christ, he is our King and Lord and Savior and Priest and Prophet and Counselor. All that he is, he is for those who are his. And then begins a life of faltering and growing yieldedness to Christ in all that he is. This can come in the form of decisive crises, or in the form of gradually growing commitment, or in the form of daily surrenderings. The lordship of Christ, in reality, is something that is not discovered and yielded to once, but thousands of times. It is yieldedness to his lordship that is at stake every time we are tempted to sin—every day.[1]

---

1. John Piper, "Letter to a Friend concerning the So-Called 'Lordship Salvation,'" Desiring God, February 1, 1990, https://www.desiringgod.org/articles/letter-to-a-friend-concerning-the-so-called-lordship-salvation.

The life of a Christian is not one that receives the benefits of Christ the Savior but later in another action receives Him as Lord. You cannot say to Jesus Christ, "You must lay aside Your power and take off Your crown before I allow You to come through my door to live in my heart, but you may bring all Your forgiveness and protecting mercy with You." Of course, you can mouth those words, but there is no way our Lord will obey you. If He is not your Lord, then please understand that He is not your Savior. You cannot come to Christ and take His benefits, scarcely stopping on your way to indulge in the things that sadly still dominate your life.

Matthew Mead, a Puritan preacher, once said,

> Many embrace Christ as a priest, but yet they own him not as a king and prophet. They like to share in his righteousness, but not to partake of his holiness. They would be redeemed by him, but they would not submit to him. They would be saved by his blood but not submit to his power. Many love the privileges of the gospel but not the duties of the gospel. These are only "almost Christians" notwithstanding they are close to Christ for that closeness is upon their own terms, but not upon God's.[2]

So who are those who come to Christ? This is another way of asking who will believe on Christ. You find in John 6 that the terms are used interchangeably,

---

2. Matthew Mead, *The Almost Christian Discovered* (Romania: Magna Gratia Ministries, 2021), 191–92.

that to believe in Christ is to come to Christ. You see it in the parallelism of verse 35: "Jesus said to them, 'I am the bread of life. He who comes to Me shall never hunger, and he who believes in Me shall never thirst.'" Again, He talks in verse 37 about the man who comes to Him not being cast out, while He says in verse 40 that he that believes in Him will be raised up. So to come to Christ is to believe in Christ, and to believe in Christ is to come to Him. So what is essentially involved in this coming and believing?

EIGHT

A True Coming Acknowledges Your Need of Christ

The first thing that a real coming to Christ will always involve is a recognition of a personal spiritual need that only Christ can meet. What does the Lord Jesus say? "Come to Me, all you who labor and are heavy laden." Burdened men and women will be among those who will come—those who have a conscious, felt, spiritual need. They might have attempted to shake it off. They might have tried immersing themselves in the pleasures of the world, but that merely increases the weight of the burden. It is the picture we are given by John Bunyan in his *Pilgrim's Progress* of a man increasingly conscious that he has a burden on his back. He is heavily laden and longs for this burden to be removed. The burden is the pilgrim's own guilt. He is like the tax collector in the temple who couldn't look up to heaven with any confidence. His eyes are fixed on the dust and he feels wretched about himself; he beats his breast and says, "God, be merciful to me a sinner" (Luke 18:13).

God has taken His law, which is the rule of life for all His creatures, the things of which He has written on a man's conscience, and in that law He says, "You are to have no other gods but Me. You are not to make an idol of anything and bow down to that thing. You are not to lace your speech with expletives and blasphemies and broken vows, taking My name in vain. Keep a day a week as special unto Me. Honor your parents. You must do no violence to your wife, to your children, to your animals, or even to your enemies. You must avoid all kinds of sexual sin, pursuing purity before marriage and faithfulness within it. You must not steal. You must not lie. You must not covet." Ten plain, wise, good words. The Holy Spirit uses them to convict men and women that by this law they are all guilty before God; not a single one of us righteous. He is a sin-hating God; He is a God who justly responds with rage at the activities of the torturer and the abuser and the thief and the drug pusher and the killer and the rapist—every single day without fail. God uses His law to light up our minds as to our condition. Conviction follows illumination.

Bunyan's pilgrim, King David, Saul of Tarsus, and the tax collector in the temple all stood in a solidarity of guilt and shame. They were laboring and heavy laden. They all knew that there was a mountain of iniquity chargeable to their account and that before them was a day of reckoning when they would face an encounter with the Judge of all the earth. How could they do anything but stand silent and guilty before Him? Their mouths were all stopped. They saw the great gulf that separated them from God. Their only hope was to come to Jesus Christ.

The Jews of our Lord's day did not have that conviction. They would not listen when John the Baptist pointed to Him and said, "Behold! The Lamb of God who takes away the sin of the world!" (John 1:29). The people would not come to Him when He invited them, even though their own Scriptures testified of a virgin-born, suffering Savior whose name was Wonderful Counselor, the Mighty God, the Everlasting Father, and Prince of Peace. Why did they keep Him at a distance? They felt they had no need of Him. They could cope without a Savior. They kept the commands and traditions. They weren't burdened by the weight of their sins. They weren't terrified by God's holy law, looking for a refuge; they weren't conscious that they were blind to the purpose of life, looking for light; they weren't conscious of the deadness of their souls, looking for life. They weren't conscious of how much they were enslaved to their sin. They weren't looking for freedom. When Jesus told them that "whosoever commits sin is the slave of sin," they said, "We are free men; we're not slaves." So He stood there, the only totally free man this world has ever seen, and they walked away from Him. They forfeited the reception of the promised rest because they rejected the divine diagnosis of their condition.

I am saying to you that you have never come to Jesus Christ in the biblical sense if you have not been made consciously aware that you've got to have His mercy, that you can't survive without Him, that He must take away the burden of your guilt and break the great chain that ties you to your past. Have you felt the weight of those heavy links dragging you down? Here is the God who is light, in whom is no darkness at all, who knows everything about your entire life—all you have done and said and also what you have failed to do and say. Your record of every deviation from His law is before Him. He is holding you accountable on the tremendous day that lies before us. And when that thought begins to press in on you, touching your conscience, awakening a sense of sin in your life, then you start to labor. "How can I be rid of this burden? To plead with God to end this life merely hastens the time I must stand before Him. I cannot run from Him. Where can I go? What bushes can hide me from the God who draws near? What fig leaves are big enough to cover my shame?" Do you know what it is to experience this? I'm not asking if you have heard preachers talking about it. Do you know what it is to experience it?

I am pressing you to answer this question as to whether the Holy Spirit has convicted you of your sin, of God's righteousness, and of the judgment to come, because when God draws near, this is what happens in an unbeliever's life. If you have never known your guilt and your need of pardon, your bondage and your need of freedom, your defilement and your need of cleansing, then how can you say that you have come to Christ? Jesus did not come for self-righteous men; He came to call sinners to turn from their sin to Him. He did not come for the healthy; He came as the Great Physician to heal sin-sick souls. He is in the business of assisting those who are sick because of sin, needy because of sin, and laboring and heavy laden because of sin. Are you such a sinner? If you deny it, then you have never come to Christ, because the first step in coming to Him is to recognize you have a need that only He can meet.

You ask whether your own conviction is merely the stirrings of a natural conscience and your need is for the Holy Spirit to come and convict you of your sin. How can you tell the difference? The natural pangs of a guilty conscience are silenced sooner or later, but the convictions wrought by the Spirit of God will not be silenced until you have come to Jesus Christ and said to Him, "God, be merciful to me a sinner." The Holy Spirit enables us to consider the sin of our nature and the nature of our sin, not simply the ways we have hurt people we love or the grief that has come to us by our transgressions. King David, when he returned to the Lord in repentance after his wickedness, cried, "Against You, You only, have I sinned, and done this evil in Your sight" (Psalm 51:4). We have sinned against God, and Spirit-wrought conviction testifies to our conscience of this.

NINE

A True Coming Recognizes Christ's Sufficiency

Didn't God refuse to spare His own Son? Then let none of us spare our own sins. John Flavel says that sin was the sword that pierced Christ, so we must let sorrow for sin pierce our hearts. If you spare sin, God will not spare you. We spare sin when we faintly oppose it; when we excuse, cover, and defend it; when we are impatient under just rebukes and reproofs. Kindness to our sins is cruelty to our own souls. The only thing to do with the sins that we have discovered is to take them with us when we go to Christ, for God the Son is the only One who can deal with the guilt and power of our sin. Everyone who comes to Him is expressing his need of Him. No one comes who has not been shown by the Holy Spirit that Christ is the perfect answer to meet his needs. How cruel it would have been for the Great Physician to diagnose the illness but then refuse to provide the cure. What would you think of a doctor who explained that the cause of your pain was cancer but then showed you to the door and told you to come back and see him the next time you find a lump? You wouldn't go to that doctor again. But this kind and loving Physician tells us what is wrong, and then He assures us that we need not fear because He possesses a cure for every sickness.

Christ is the light that illuminates our path through life. He is a wall of fire to defend us. He is the friend to comfort us, the counselor to advise us, the garment to clothe our nakedness, the diamond to enrich us, the foundation to build on, the ark to deliver us from the flood, the vaccine to save us from the cosmic pandemic of a fallen world, a refuge from the storm, a spring of water in a dry land. He is the ladder between earth and heaven, the Mediator between man and God.

What treasures are His—boundless, unfathomable, inexhaustible. Your debts, however vast, are not too great for Christ to meet. Judge your need only by His abundance. He has immeasurable resources to spare: He has food enough to feed both you and yours throughout their lives, wisdom enough to solve your perplexities, comfort enough to soothe your sorrows and drive away your fears, blood enough to wash away your guilt and fully pardon your most shameful act, righteousness enough to justify you, grace enough to strengthen and sanctify you. That is why you have come to Him alone, at His invitation, and find sufficiency in Him. That is the greatest discovery anyone can ever make.

Listen to Samuel Rutherford, who came to Christ and discovered that He met all his needs:

> O, what a fair One, what an only One, what an
> excellent, lovely, ravishing One is Jesus. Put the

beauty of ten thousand, thousand worlds of paradises, like the garden of Eden in one, put all trees, all flowers, all smells, all colors, all tastes, all joys, all sweetness, all loveliness, in one.... And yet it would be less to that fair and dearest well-beloved Christ, than one drop of rain to the whole seas, rivers, lakes, and fountains of ten thousand earths.

Every day we may see some new thing in Christ. His love has neither brim nor bottom. How blessed are we to enjoy this invaluable treasure, the love of Christ; or rather allow ourselves to be mastered and subdued in his love, so that Christ is our all, and all other things are nothing. O that we might be ready for the time our Lord's wind and tide call for us!

There are infinite supplies in his love that the saint will never be able to unfold. I urge upon you a nearer and growing communion with Christ. There are curtains to be drawn back in Christ that we have never seen. There are new unfoldings of love in him. Dig deep, sweat, labour, and take pains for him, and set by as much time in the day for him as you can; he will be won with that commitment. Live on Christ's love.

Christ's love is so kingly, that it will not wait until tomorrow, it must have a throne all alone in your soul. It is our folly to divide and keep our narrow and little love. It is best to give it all to Christ. Lay no more on the earthly, than it can carry. Lay your soul and your weights upon God; make him your only and best-beloved. Your errand in this life is to make sure an eternity of glory for your soul, and to match your soul with Christ. Your love, if it could be more than all the love of angels in one, would be Christ's due. Look up to him and love him. O, love and live! Come to him![1]

It is in the discovery of the inexhaustible riches of Christ that we make discovery of this One to whom we have come. This is where the enemy of our souls will try with all his skill to lead us astray, lest we should discover what Samuel Rutherford found. This is when the most terrible mistakes are made. This is where the greatest religious blunders take place. The devil is most active when men and women are no longer careless and indifferent about their sins but are seriously searching for the truth. He will send them anywhere and to any-thing—to mind-altering drugs, psychiatrists, religious rituals, transcendental meditation—rather than send them to the Lord Jesus Christ, though He alone is the One who can meet their need!

Jesus Christ is the inviting Savior who says, "No, you must come to Me—not to men, not to your past, not to church and the ordinances, but to Me alone." This is the One to whom you must come—the only person who obeyed the law perfectly and so had no sins of His own to make atonement for so that He could become your substitute and lay down His life in your stead. Christ died for our sins. Paul says He "loved me and gave Himself for me" (Galatians 2:20). He alone can deal with all your burden of sin. He will pardon all of it—all your

1. Samuel Rutherford, *The Loveliness of Christ* (Louisville, Ky.: G. L. H. Publishers, 2016), 40.

past sins, all your present sins, and all your future sins. He is perfectly suited to meet your needs.

How do we know that such a wonder is working in Jesus's death on Calvary? It is because of His resurrection on the third day. God raised Him from the dead. The resurrection took place in human history, in space and time. A stone was rolled away, and He came out more powerful than death, announcing that the grave and the corpse rotting in it is not ultimate reality. That is Jesus: He who put to death the power of death, He who made reconciliation with God by His death, He who dealt with our guilt and blame by taking it on Himself on Golgotha's cross. We must go to Him. To whom else can we go? He lives, and if He invites, then why should we stay away?

I see how perfect He is to be my Teacher, to tell me where this world came from, who God is, why our land is in the state it's in, why men behave as foully as they do, what is man's chief end, what I must do to be saved, how I should live, what sort of man or woman I should be, what sort of husband and father, what sort of wife and mother. Jesus Christ will teach me in His Word.

I see how perfect He is to be my Great High Priest. The living God requires atonement; without the shedding of blood there is no forgiveness of sins. That is how God functions. That is His nature. But He who requires sacrifice provides the sacrifice: the Lamb is found in God's flock. God gave His only begotten Son to make atonement for sin. He who died to forgive us our sins now is risen and lives at the right hand of God as our mediator. He makes intercession for us and so can save us to the uttermost.

I see how perfect the Lord Jesus is to be my sovereign protector. He is my good shepherd. He determines that if anything affects me in any way, it must work for my good. He puts it under an unbreakable obligation to work for my good, both the best things that happen to me and the worst things. He keeps me from being overwhelmed by the temptations of the world—the lust of the eyes and the lust of the flesh and the pride of life. He gives me armor that enables me to know protection from the devices and attacks of the devil. Nothing can separate me from His love. He has determined that where He is, there I will also be one day. The Lord Jesus Christ is perfectly suitable to meet all my needs in this world and the next. All that we need we shall find in Christ. If we want little, we shall find little. If we want much, we shall find much. But if, in utter helplessness, we cast our all on Christ, He will be to us the whole treasury of God.

TEN

A True Coming Results in a Credible, Sincere Commitment

The final and indispensable aspect of coming to Christ always involves a resignation to Him. Coming to our Lord is a movement of the heart as the Holy Spirit uses the truths we have outlined to motivate the very center of our being, that dispositional complex of self-consciousness and intelligence and feeling out of which all the issues of life flow. So I come to Jesus Christ keeping back nothing. I put myself in His hands. I place myself under the atoning covering of His death. My one plea for God accepting me is that Jesus Christ, God's own Son, has lived and died for me. I bow before Him as my Lord and my God. I resign myself to Him: "Your will be done on earth as it is in heaven" (Matthew 6:10).

"Take my life and let it be consecrated, Lord, to Thee." I go through all the specifics of that great hymn— take my life, my moments, my days, my hands, my feet, my voice, my lips, my silver and my gold, my intellect, my will, my heart, and my love. I commit myself, just as I am, to Him who invites me to come—entirely and without reservation, body and soul, for time and eternity. That is coming to Christ. As Dr. John Piper says,

> If I say to God in prayer, "O Lord, I give myself to You," what I mean is this: I am saying a very earnest, heartfelt "Yes!" to God's purchase of me by the death of his Son so that I belong to him. He purchased me so that I belong to him, not only by virtue of his paying a price for me, but also by virtue of my willing surrender to him. That's what I'm doing when I say, "I give myself to you." I'm saying, "I'm no longer my owner, my master, my shepherd. You are my Owner, Master, Shepherd, Father, my treasure, my wisdom, my hope, my source of fullest and lasting pleasure. I renounce finding all of that in me. I look for it now in you, because I am utterly yours."[1]

There is nothing I am or that I possess of which I can say, "But this is exclusively mine and not God's. I can do with this just as I please." No, He is my master, and I am His bondservant; He can deal with me just as He pleases. I give everything to Him.

There was once a student in our congregation who was an earnest Christian. His hobby was his camera, and he had fine equipment and a gift for photography. One day he told me he was selling it all because it had too great a hold over his life. I urged him to think again and that it was perfectly legitimate for a Christian to have an interest like photography, or music, or walking

---

1. Piper, "Letter to a Friend."

in the country, but he insisted that it had too strong a hold over his life. I was concerned he was becoming a little extreme in his discipleship. Over twenty years later he and his wife were on holiday in Wales, and one day they came to visit, both of them strong in the Lord. At the end of the visit, he took out his camera to take our photograph. I noticed what a fine camera he had. He had given up his photography to Jesus Christ so that he might serve Him with all his heart, and do you see the Savior did nothing to prevent him from making this gesture? Then there came a time when he was stronger in the faith and the Lord gave it back to him, knowing now that it was not going to be his master but his servant, used to the glory of God. Thus it is with everything that might become a rival or an idol that will take our fascination, our time, and our money. We give it all to the Lord and let Him judge for how long. Whatever God gives to us, He gives freely, and whatever He takes from us, He takes justly. So when God is free to give, let us be at peace about it, and whenever God is just to take, let us be free to resign. And when God gives us something—a talent, a delight, a friendship, a possession—then let us receive it with thankfulness and use it to His glory and our happy enjoyment.

In all of God's dealings with us as His children, He is teaching us that our highest goal in Christian discipleship is to say with contentment, "May I keep this? Nevertheless, not my will but Yours be done." Nothing is gained by struggling against the will of God, nor anything lost by quietly submitting to Him. We are to be lions in serving the cause of God but lambs in serving our own cause. The less any man strives to serve his own cause, the more he is acknowledging that God is his chief executive officer!

ELEVEN

How Will You Respond?

So you are still reading this book and now have come to the penultimate chapter. What encouragement to know that you have come with me so far. You know the reason for this? The living God and Father of our Lord Jesus Christ desires you to come to the Savior, and so He is encouraging you to learn about the way you can truly come to Christ. This is His invitation to you right now, this very minute. He is saying to you, "'As I live,' says the Lord GOD, 'I have no pleasure in the death of the wicked, but that the wicked turn from his way and live'" (Ezekiel 33:11). He is saying now, "'Come now, and let us reason together,' says the LORD, 'Though your sins are like scarlet, they shall be as white as snow; though they are red like crimson, they shall be as wool'" (Isaiah 1:18).

I have been a part of His kind providence toward you in that He helped me to write this little book and then through various good and mysterious means He brought it into your hands. Its message is the most wonderful good news for one outstanding reason: because it is true. I have told you what the Creator of the universe has done for people just like you. He knew your guilt; He foresaw that you would ruin yourself. He knew that His justice would demand your blood, and in order that this difficulty might be escaped, that His justice might have its full due, and that yet you might be saved, Jesus Christ, the Lamb of God, has died and risen.

There He was on His knees in the garden of Gethsemane, sweating drops of blood. There He was, tied to a pillar and lashed with a terrible scourging whip until, no doubt, His shoulder bones were seen like white islands in the midst of a sea of blood. There He was, hanging on the cross with hands extended and feet nailed fast, dying, groaning, bleeding until crying out loudly and triumphantly, "It is finished." All this Jesus Christ of Nazareth has done in order that God might be consistent in exercising absolute justice, hating our wickedness yet pardoning sin.

You have received a divine warrant to respond now by coming to Jesus Christ. God is commanding and inviting you to do so. It is decision time, a commitment of yourself just as you are to the living Christ who is watching and waiting. "Believe on the Lord Jesus Christ, and you will be saved" (Acts 16:31). That is, entrust yourself to Him alone. Set your heart alone on this man, who gave Himself for sinners like you and me.

So what is your response? I hope that it is this:

Just as I am, without one plea
But that Thy blood was shed for me
And that Thou bid'st me come to Thee
O Lamb of God, I come!

Just as I am, though tossed about
With many a conflict, many a doubt
Fighting and fears within, without,
O Lamb of God, I come!

Just as I am, and waiting not
To rid my soul of one dark blot
To thee whose blood can cleanse each spot
O Lamb of God, I come!

Just as I am, poor, wretched, blind
Sight, riches, healing of the mind
Yea, all I need, in Thee to find
O Lamb of God, I come!

But you may be uncertain and suggest particular reasons for not coming. Let me speak to your reservations. What is the first?

1. "I will think about it."

You may return to this book and read it again, but now you think there are important things you have to do. There are studies to attend to, meals to prepare, shops to visit, favorite programs to watch, work you have brought home that you have to complete, emails to write, weeding in the garden calls for you, and it is past your time for going to bed. Stop! I told you from the beginning that your coming to Christ was not while you were on your way to any or all of those tasks. No. I have brought you to the Christ who is saying to you, "Come to Me!" And so I want to encourage you to come and stay before this Christ and terminate any distance there has been, large or small, between you and Him by coming just as you are and standing before Him with your questions and imperfect faith.

I am speaking to you now. I am so thankful that you read this book. You have honored me by doing that, but it was God's help that kept you reading until now. Please stop a moment longer before other pleasant tasks call you away. Do not shrug off any stirrings you have felt in your mind and heart! The time has now come for you to end this period in your life of almost being a Christian. You may never be closer to God than you are this moment. Do not presume on a time when things will seem clearer, when your desire for God will be greater, or when other things will not be pressing on you for your attention. I speak to you in the name of my Lord and urge you to heed His invitation and His commandment to you to come to the Lord Jesus Christ.

You say you won't be commanded? Then again will I change my note. I *exhort* you to flee across the gap that lies between you and Christ. Run! Jump into His outstretched arms. Oh, my friend, don't you know what a loving Christ He is? In my own experience there were many Sunday nights that I heard the invitations to run to a loving Savior. He knocked at the door of my heart, and I refused to open it. He came to me times without number; He checked me in my conscience and spoke to me by His Spirit. Then what a loving reception I had when I went to Him. His eyes were full of tears. He fell on my neck and kissed me. He took off my rags and clothed me with His righteousness. He gave me joy and assurance of salvation. I finally exhort you, then, that you should come to Jesus Christ. You will never regret it. Though tempted to go back into the world, you will be embraced by a love that will not let you go. You will occasionally find the trials of Christian living very heavy, but you will find compensating grace that will give you rest, His yoke being easy and His burden being light. There are such joys and delights from knowing you are a child of God. You will taste and see that the Lord is good. I am not afraid to promise that you shall find He's not only good but is better than human lips can ever describe.

Are you happy living without God, not knowing what life is all about, carrying the burden of your guilt for the ways you have hurt the people who love you the most? What are you getting by staying away from Christ? I exhort you by everything that is important and eternal. The cross of Christ has achieved your reconciliation with a holy God. Then start to speak to Him. Tell Him of your doubts. Bring your cares and questions. Come to Jesus Christ! I *entreat* you to stop and consider.

Do you know what it is you are rejecting today? You are rejecting the Creator of the heavens and the earth. You are rejecting the One who rose from the dead on the third day. You also may be rejecting the most preciously held views of those who brought this book to you. You are rejecting the One who has given you friends who love you and have prayed long for you to come to Jesus Christ. And the mighty Maker of heaven and earth actually wants you to come to Him now, and He will be your loving friend and wise counselor forevermore.

You know what lies inescapably before you, don't you? You are going to die. One day you will breathe your last breath. My saying it is not going to bring it a minute sooner, but neither will your refusal to speak about it, let alone think about it, put it off a minute later. It is appointed unto men and women once to die. When I was a wee eight-year-old boy, the thought of being in my eighties seemed a vast period of time away. I want to tell you from my pilgrimage that it is but a moment. Death is not a thing to ignore. I should be worse than a fiend if I did not now, with all love, kindness, and earnestness, beseech you to come to Christ and lay hold of eternal life. I tell you not to put it off. Here is a day of grace—there is no guarantee you will have another.

2. "I do not feel worthy of coming to Christ."

I can understand that feeling. I have some wonderful friends, and I often feel that if they really knew me—if they could read my thoughts and imaginations—they would spit in my face. I am unworthy of their affection. But this extraordinary friend Jesus Christ seeks your friendship while knowing all about you, even those things that make you groan and sigh. He even knows all your subsequent falls in the years ahead. They will not be a surprise to Him. He still invites you to come. You say that you have been far worse than me. Maybe.

That is your guess. You protest, "But, sir, I feel that I have been the chief of sinners." Friend, you are not. The chief of sinners died and went to heaven many years ago; his name was Saul of Tarsus, afterward called Paul the apostle. He was the chief of sinners, and I know he spoke the truth. "No," you are rejecting my words still, "I am too vile." You cannot be viler than the *chief* of sinners. You must, at least, be second worst. But suppose you are the worst. Isn't that a great reason why you should come to Christ? The best reason, of course, is that He is sincerely inviting you now to come to Him. He is showing friendship to you while knowing everything about you. The sicker a man is, the more reason he should go to a doctor. The poorer you are, the more reason you should accept the generosity of another. Now, Christ does not demand any merits of yours. He gives freely. The worse you are, the more welcome you are.

OK. You are unworthy. Join the club! Not a single worthy person has come to Christ. We all have sinned and fallen short of the glory of God. Let me ask you a question: Do you think you will ever get better by refusing to come to Christ? No way! The longer you stay away, the worse you will grow. Your hope will grow weaker, your despair will become stronger, the nail with which Satan has fastened you down will be more firmly hammered in, and you will be less hopeful than ever. Come to Christ! There is nothing to be gained by delay, but by delay everything may be lost.

3. "I have tried to come to Him, but I cannot believe."

That is true. No man can come to Christ unless the Father who first sent His Son also draws you to Him. But how does God draw us to Christ? He sends His Spirit into your heart and illuminates your mind so that you begin to understand the greatness and grace of Jesus Christ. His Spirit begins to show you the loveliness of Christ, removing the scarf that covers your eyes and makes you a blind man. He brings the gospel to you in a book, or by a preacher, or through a meeting of people. He grips your interest and gives you understanding and starts to draw you to Christ. And as that is the case, why are you not praying to Him to draw you? Why not acknowledge your impotence to come unaided? Plead with Him that you cannot come without His grace, and don't stop until you know He is answering you. Cast yourself on His pity. Plead His invitations to you now and cry, "Give me a day of Your power and make me one who has come to Your Son."

You say you cannot believe, but you never will believe if your eyes are fixed on your believing. This book is not about inviting you to faith but about coming to Christ. You say, "What's the difference?" Why, it is just this question: Did your faith live for you? Did your faith die for and rise for you? Does your faith plead at God's right hand for your salvation? That is Christ, isn't it? Our first business hasn't to do with faith, but with Christ. Come to Him, I beseech you, and see the cross. Behold the Son of God, dying for our sins. Isn't there

power in such an incarnate God to save? Look at His
face so full of pity. Is there not love in His heart that
proves He is able and *willing* to save? Doubt no more!
It is the spiritual sight of the Christ of the Bible, not a
certainty that we have faith, that helps us to come to
Him. We do not believe first, then come to Christ. Come
to Christ without any faith, and cast yourself on Him.

4. "How many times I have heard the gospel and rejected the Lord! I am now gospel hardened."

I do not know anything about you; all I know is that
my Master has given me grace to write this little book
about coming to His Son, Jesus Christ, for eternal life. It
is time for you to come. You may have rejected a thousand invitations—don't choose to make this a thousand
and one. You say you have been up to the house of God
and have only been gospel hardened by the visit. But
does God detect now some restlessness and a new seed
of longing? Are you asking for an oak tree? But hasn't
God planted in your heart an acorn? It is enough. If
your faith is lodged in Christ, it is saving faith. We are
not saved because of our faith. We are saved because of
Christ. We are joined to Him by coming and, as it were,
by reaching out and touching the hem of His garment.
Tell the enemy of your soul that you are not going to
listen to him when he says you cannot come because
you have hardened your heart. One greater than your
heart is speaking, and His voice deafens the voice of the
devil. He says, "Ignore Satan and come to Me." I cannot let you go on with idle excuses. If you have lived so

many years slighting Christ, there are so many reasons why now you should never slight Him again.

But maybe you are being too hard on yourself. There are some sensitive Christians who find their faith weak and wonder if they really are disciples of Christ. They feel the power of remaining sin, their doubts, and their vainglory with shame. But often God sees more grace in His sin-burdened people than they see in themselves. Abraham's wife refused to believe the promises of God, but her submission to her husband was noted by God. On the last day, the Lord Jesus will commend His people for good works that they have long forgotten and that they struggle even to recognize. His "Well done!" says much of the wonder of His mercy. Can you say, "I don't know if I have Him, but I know this—that if I had Him, I'd be safe"? Only someone who has truly come to Christ thinks like that.

5. "It is not a convenient time."

It is always inconvenient to come to Christ. Every worldling has a full timetable. When will that convenient time come to you? Shall it come when you are in hell? Will that time be convenient? Shall it come when you are on your dying bed? When the painkillers make you drowsy and your memory is failing, will that be a convenient time to think of salvation through Jesus Christ? No. Today, while you're reading this book, is the convenient time for you. May God make it so. Remember, I have no authority to ask you to come to Christ *tomorrow*. The Master has given you no invitation to come to

Him next Tuesday. The invitation is *"Today,* if you will listen to what He is saying, do not harden your heart." The Spirit of God is saying, "Come *now* and let us reason together." Why should you put it off? It could be the last warning you might ever have. Put it off, and you may never weep again for your soul and your sin and a Savior's love. You may never read so earnest a book again. You may not be pleaded with to consider the claims of Christ as I am pleading with you now. You may from this moment on go further and further away, and God may say, "He is given to his idols, let him alone." May it not be so!

TWELVE

Come Now to an Inviting Lord and Never Cease Coming

Surely all this is not to be in vain? You have read these pages and thought about their message, and still you won't come to Christ? Then what more can I do? I have but one more resort. I can pray for you as I end this book: "Lord, You know who will take this book in their hands and read it all the way through. You see and hear them in the future as You see and hear me now praying that these words will be new life and a new love for You in the reading of one person in particular, and in many more." I have brought you into the orbit of the merciful Father in heaven, the redeeming Son, and the life-giving Holy Spirit. You may scorn these pages as difficult, boring, and wearying. You can mock my style or say I must be a fanatic. But I will never hear your comments, and I won't chide. I will bring no accusation against you to the great Judge. Your offense, so far as I am concerned, is forgiven before it is committed. But do not forget this: Once you discovered a book that somehow came into your hands. It was written by someone who had good news to tell you of the love of God and the offer of eternal life and forgiveness from the God who is light. And though we have never met, you have met others in my huge family of faith, my brothers and sisters, one of whom might have given you this book and recommended it to you out of love. You may make jokes about the devil and the hell that is his dwelling place, thinking all this is a matter of no importance. But there are one or two of us who are in earnest about your soul and your eternity and your God.

Young people, maybe you do not pray for yourselves, but your mothers bring you to the throne of grace and pray for you day after day for decades. You may not think of your own souls, but your parents' anxiety is focused on you. I have been at prayer meetings and heard Christians pray, and they could not have prayed with more earnestness and more intensity of anguish if they had been seeking their own soul's salvation. And is it not strange that those in the family of faith should be ready to move heaven and earth for your salvation yet you should have no thought for *yourselves*, no regard to eternal things?

Does anything else remain to the disciple of Jesus Christ besides writing and praying? He can now appeal to the Spirit. I know I have explained the gospel, that I have written about it earnestly, and so I call on my Master to honor His own promise. He has said that what He declares shall not return unto Him void. It is in His hands, not mine. I cannot compel you, but Jesus Christ has the key of the heart, and He can not only constrain but open the heart. In the book of Revelation, the Lord Jesus speaks and says, "Behold, I stand at the door and knock" (3:20). But if knocking brings no response, He has the key, and He can and will open the heart and enter. Every page you have turned is a knock on the door. It is the Son of God who is knocking. I pray that He will open the door and give you life forever. May His sovereign grace draw you today to His Son. In finding Him you will know life, love, joy, and peace eternally.